INTRODUCTION TO
PASTORAL COUNSELING

Introduction to Pastoral Counseling

Loren Townsend

Abingdon Press
Nashville

INTRODUCTION TO PASTORAL COUNSELING

This book is printed on acid-free paper.

Library of Congress Cataloging-in-Publication Data

Townsend, Loren L.
  Introduction to pastoral counseling / Loren Townsend.
    p. cm.
  Includes bibliographical references.
  ISBN 978-0-687-65835-0 (binding: adhesive- lay-flat binding : alk. paper)
  1. Pastoral counseling.   I. Title.

  BV4012.2.T69 2008
  253.5—dc22

2008042198

09 10 11 12 13 14 15 16 17 18—10 9 8 7 6 5 4 3 2 1

MANUFACTURED IN THE UNITED STATES OF AMERICA

To my colleague and spouse, Leslie Smith Townsend, PhD, MFA, who interrupts her own schedule to read what I write, tells me when I miss the mark, enthusiastically reminds me of what I must do to be a better writer, and assures that our house does not collapse while my attention is consumed by the task

Contents

Introduction

Writing an introduction to pastoral counseling has never been first on my list of things to do. Yet I was attracted to the task for three reasons. First, I could find no contemporary text that introduced students to the complexities of today's pastoral counseling in a way that satisfied me. Consequently, this text is first and foremost written to my students. It is an introduction to the field rather than a "how to" counseling book. It replaces (at least in part) the collage of book chapters, journal articles, and essays I usually construct anytime I introduce the field. Second, I have now lived through nearly thirty years of pastoral counseling history. The field has changed substantially. The books that introduced me to the field do not capture the breadth of change that has redefined pastoral counseling's institutional life, intellectual foundations, and clinical practices. Part of my motive here is to observe and interpret some of the important changes that have redefined the pastoral counseling movement. Finally, I wrote this text as a way to report research findings of a three-year grounded theory study titled "What's Pastoral about Pastoral Counseling? A Grounded Theory Study" (identified as WPC in the following chapters). This study was funded initially (2005) by a Lilly Research Costs Grant. A later (2006) grant from the American Association of Pastoral Counselors' (AAPC) Mission Advance Program allowed me to continue the project. These motives are reflected in three primary goals: (1) to provide a general historic overview of pastoral counseling; (2) to offer a critical analysis of pastoral counseling as a contemporary field of study and set of clinical practices; and (3) as much as possible, to ground my description and analysis in empirical sources. The third goal, to use empirical sources, has pressed me to observe pastoral counseling as it is expressed in actual practice and as it engages other contemporary sources of theological, behavioral science, and psychotherapeutic knowledge. Out of this mix grows a vision of pastoral counseling as a diverse field tentatively feeling its way into *multiversal*[1] existence in a complex and plural world. Pastoral counseling is not what it once was, and it is not yet what it will eventually be.

I wrote this text as a particular kind of observer. I am observing the field of which I have been a part for most of my professional life. I am a participant-observer in the qualitative research project that provided much of the data for this text. My observations are filtered through my social location: I am a white, male, baby boomer, seminary-educated, ordained Baptist minister who teaches in a Presbyterian seminary. I am a clinician, supervisor, and researcher. I was a marriage and family therapist before entering seminary and discovering pastoral counseling. I entered pastoral counseling "sideways," without the benefit or constrictions of traditional pastoral counselor training, but have taught in AAPC-approved programs for most of my twenty-nine years as a pastoral counselor. My vantage is influenced by the fact that my seminary training was preceded and followed by graduate study in research-heavy universities. It is also affected by the fact that my own formation is rooted in liberation and postmodern theologies rather than neo-orthodox, contemporary evangelical, or existential theologies. My history with psychotherapy is broad but has centered in social constructionist approaches over the past twenty years. I am likely to attend to how meaning (and theory) is constructed in particular social locations and to be skeptical of invariant, universal claims to knowledge made by either theology or psychotherapy theory. Consequently, when I describe pastoral counseling in the following pages, I tend to value a blend of empirical and narrative descriptive procedures.

Rather than theoretically or theologically describing what pastoral counseling should be, I have tried to achieve what qualitative researchers call a "thick description" of pastoral counseling as it is manifest in pastoral counselors' practices and as it intersects with the behavioral sciences. Part of this is accomplished by literature review and part by result of "What's Pastoral about Pastoral Counseling? A Grounded Theory Study." A full description of this project and its results is beyond my purpose here. However, since

I am asking readers to trust the study in the following chapters, it seems important briefly to define grounded theory and describe enough of this study's procedures to instill confidence.

Grounded theory is a research strategy designed to study people and processes in their natural context.[2] It is a method to investigate how meanings, such as those associated with pastoral counseling, are created, understood, and used. As a research strategy, it uses constant-comparison to examine raw data (interviews and written statements in this case) and discover concepts and relationships that can be organized into an explanatory framework. Qualitative research, which includes grounded theory, does not rely on statistical analysis of large, random samples that can be generalized to a larger population. Instead, it studies smaller samples and tries to understand them in depth by expanding the sample and collecting data until interviews or other methods produce no new information. It makes no claim that results can be generalized, though it does assume that patterns found in natural environments tend to be repeated. Because qualitative research does not rely on statistical analysis to establish truthfulness and in some cases statistical references can be misleading, I have avoided descriptions using percentages or other mathematical descriptions. Instead, I will use more general terms such as *many, most,* or *more than half* to communicate the descriptive rather than statistically precise nature of grounded theory. This study (WPC) collected interviews or written statements from eighty-five pastoral counselors selected for maximum variation of religious affiliation, race, gender, ethnicity, geographic location, sexual orientation, social class, training history, and location of current practice. Validity in qualitative research rests on truthfulness. In this study, truthfulness was achieved by collecting data in multiple ways, using focus groups of pastoral counselors to review emerging analysis, reviewing data with colleagues, and actively seeking interviews that could contradict the emerging explanatory framework.

The following chapters are organized into two sections. The first section, "Contexts—Who Are Pastoral Counselors?" describes the historical and contemporary contexts in which pastoral counseling must be understood. Chapter 1 follows a genealogical trail from ancient practices of care and describes how pastoral counseling emerged in the twentieth century as a psychotherapeutically based ministry. Chapter 2 revisits this genealogy and presents a painful analysis of how the history of pastoral counseling reflects the deep racial segregation of American churches. This chapter explores how stories and contributions of people of color have been subjugated by Euro-American dominance in the field. Chapter 3 establishes a contemporary context for pastoral counseling by evaluating changes over the past two decades and describing how the field is diversifying in a pluralistic context. Section II, "Practices—What Do Pastoral Counselors Do?" relies on literature review and grounded theory research to describe contemporary pastoral counseling practice, its relationship to behavioral science and psychotherapy, and its use of theological resources. Chapter 4 explores four ways counselors bring together behavioral sciences and theology, or psychotherapy and spirituality. Where a pastoral counselor "fits" in these methods largely determines a pastoral counselor's attitude about psychotherapeutic theory and how she or he will use it as part of her or his practice. Chapter 5 examines how pastoral counselors use therapeutic relationships to promote transformation and relates this to recent research in psychotherapy and change. Doing this is especially challenging now that hundreds of psychotherapy models are available. Rather than selecting favorite theories to organize this chapter, my approach is pan-theoretical and examines how pastoral counselors can use psychotherapeutic theory flexibly and match client need to pastoral relationship, empathy, and therapeutic procedures. Chapter 6 describes how pastoral counselors reflect theologically and ethically on their work. It provides a picture of pastoral counseling as a discipline guided by a theological framework. Here I describe a model of liberative praxis useful for organizing pastoral counseling goals and procedures with particular attention to how theological reflection can be integrated into postmodern models of psychotherapy. Readers are encouraged to examine endnotes for each chapter. These contain definitions and expanded explanations as well as reference citations.

Finally, I need to say a word about case studies and quotations. Pastoral counselors promise confidentiality to clients and research participants. To protect confidentiality, I have left quotations from research participants anonymous. When a number of people have said the same thing, I used a composite to capture meaning without citing each variation on a similar theme. Because there may be only one or two pastoral counselors in the country from a particular religious or ethnic group, I have taken greater care to disguise comments from these participants without altering meaning. Except in chapter 2, case studies are composites to illustrate how pastoral counselors manage their practice. While they represent actual clinical work, case studies are constructed in ways that protect client confidentiality. Quotations and case studies in chapter 2 reflect actual statements made by pastoral counselors.

I want to thank the pastoral counselors who participated in the research that made this book possible, and the Lilly Foundation and the American Association of Pastoral Counselors for funding the study that grounds it. I also want to thank students who have taught me so much over the years and motivated me to write this book. Thanks also to the Board of Trustees, faculty, staff, and students of Louisville Presbyterian Theological Seminary, who provide support and a creative context for research and writing.

Notes

1. *Multiverse* is a term used by Humberto Maturana to describe the idea that human knowledge is not singular and universal. Experience has many possible meanings, and there are many possible pictures of the world.

2. A. Strauss and J. Corbin, *Basics of Qualitative Research: Techniques and Procedures for Developing Grounded Theory* (Thousand Oaks, Calif.: Sage, 1998); Barney Glaser and Anselm Strauss, *The Discovery of Grounded Theory* (Hawthorne, N.Y.: Aldine De Gruyter, 1967).

SECTION I

Contexts: Who Are Pastoral Counselors?

CHAPTER 1

Pastoral Counseling: A Genealogy

The *Dictionary of Pastoral Care and Counseling* defines pastoral counseling as a twentieth-century phenomenon. It emerged among North American Protestant pastors who incorporated new psychological information into their ministries, and by midcentury it had become a ministry specialty requiring distinctive training.[1] However, pastoral counselors claim a genealogy anchored in ancient Hebrew and Christian understanding of care, expanded through the history of the Western Christian church and the Protestant Reformation, and later focused in the confluence of modern theology and behavioral sciences in late nineteenth-century Europe and North America. This genealogy highlights contemporary pastoral counseling's Euro-American characteristics and the dominant Protestant, clerical interpretive tradition that anchors its identity. It also shows that pastoral care and counseling were central factors in shaping congregational life and clergy practice in American history. Equally important, historical review helps us appreciate what practices, traditions, and people are marginalized or excluded by the particularity of this genealogy.

Context: Judeo-Christian Care of the Soul

In his *Introduction to Pastoral Care*, Charles Gerkin noted that structured care and counseling extends "back as far as the collective memories of the Christian community can be extended."[2] This foundation has sustained care and counseling for nearly two millennia. He observed that the oldest Judeo-Christian model of care rests on a threefold tradition. Prophets, priests, and wise women and men were responsible for helping God's people organize life effectively. Each had a unique focus—prophets assured continuity of tradition, priests organized worship, and wise men and women provided practical guidance in daily life. The constancy of these three elements through history led Gerkin to conclude that care of God's people always rests in a "trialogical tension and interaction" among these three central elements of care. This tension was consolidated in Jesus, "the good shepherd." Central to the Gospel of John, this metaphor depicts Jesus' ministry as the unified expression of wisdom (parables), prophetic action (cleansing of the temple), and priestly leadership (relationship with his followers). It was a metaphor so compelling that "shepherd of the flock" became the prototypical image of a pastor in the early church.

The Synoptic Gospels contain details of Jesus' ministry that anticipate pastoral counseling practices. In *A History of the Cure of Souls*, John McNeill[3] observed that synoptic writers emphasize Jesus' difference from other scribes, rabbis, teachers, and masters of wisdom. While he was sometimes called Rabbi (and may have had rabbinic training), Jesus appears most often as a healer of souls who conversationally engaged male and female disciples, public leaders, and moral outcasts. Unlike other religious leaders, his ministry was marked by a clear focus on human need and God's care for those who suffer. Instead of gathering large crowds intentionally, Jesus seemed to prefer transformational conversations with individuals or small groups. These were often structured to encourage lively dialogue that led others to discover important truths, or to offer spiritual renewal and rest. McNeill pointed to gospel stories such as the rich ruler (Mark 10:17-22), Zacchaeus (Luke 19:1-10), Jesus' encounter with the Syrophoenecian woman (Matt 15:21-28), his conversation with Nicodemus (John 3:1-10), and his encounter with the Samaritan woman (John 4:7-14) as characteristic of Jesus' personal, conversational approach.

Jesus' example as "good shepherd" was carried into the early church by pastors who responded personally to human need. Their interventions nurtured and protected Christian faith and offered guidance for living. The Apostle Paul expressed this through his "anxiety for all the churches" (2 Cor 11:28), which motivated him frequently to provide practical—and sometimes very personal—guidance to congregations and individual church leaders. His letters are rich with examples of pastoral responses to specific prob-

4

lems. These included, for example, questions of sexual ethics (1 Cor 7:1-9), decision making in situations of personal difference (Rom 14:2-12), personal failure and depression (2 Cor 1:8, 11), marital problems (Eph 4–5), divorce (1 Cor 7:10-16), self-destructive lifestyles (1 Cor 5:4-6; 2 Cor 2:5-11; Gal 6:1), and mutual support within the community of believers (Rom 14:7, 15, 19; 1 Thess 5:11). Paul's personal greetings expressed care for individuals and showed that he often knew the cast of characters in an unfolding drama. His interventions addressed specific personalities and interpreted the local context of specific problems.

In their analysis of pastoral care, Clebsch and Jaekle[4] note that through most of Christian history, *pastoral* has described a specific constellation "of helping acts, done by *representative Christian persons,* directed toward the *healing, sustaining, guiding,* and *reconciling* of *troubled persons* whose troubles arise *in the context of ultimate meanings and concerns*" (italics in original). Care begins when an individual[5] experiencing an insoluble problem that exhausts personal resources turns to a person who represents the resources, wisdom, and authority of religion. This person need not be clergy or an official representative of a faith tradition. However, *pastoral* does specifically require one who offers care to be grounded in the resources of a specific faith tradition, to have access to the wisdom generated by the heritage of Christians' experience, and to be able to claim the authority of a "company of believers." This foundation allows a pastoral carer to engage troubled persons at the point of deepest meaning. Deep religious meaning and ultimate concerns are often hidden or unconscious. Pastoral carers must have skills to respond to ultimate concerns that are expressed implicitly through problems in living.

Clebsch and Jaekle identify four basic functions of pastoral care that emerged in the early church (healing, sustaining, guiding, and reconciling) and trace how these are variously emphasized through eight "epochs" of Western church history. For instance, while examples of all four functions can be found in records of care from the period of church persecution (and again in Reformation years), pastors were more often concerned with reconciliation than with healing, guiding, or sustaining. On the other hand, guiding took a focal role in the period of church consolidation after Constantine and during the Dark Ages. The medieval church codified care in a sacramental system to emphasize illness and healing. During the Enlightenment, care was organized around sustaining souls in a treacherous world, and care in post-Christendom (late eighteenth and nineteenth centuries) emphasized pluralism, voluntarism, and guidance toward personal value systems and norms. Charles Gerkin appropriates this epochal story of Western Christian history to develop his thesis that pastoral care is always formed in a specific social location that must balance four tensions. Care must attend (1) to the foundational tradition that grounds faith and practice within the Christian community, (2) to the life of the community of faith itself, (3) to the needs and problems of individuals and families, and (4) to the "issues and concerns of the contemporary cultural context."[6] Pastoral care, Gerkin asserts, is always culturally situated and shaped by the interaction of these factors in particular times and places. American history provided a unique context that helped shape pastoral counseling into a twentieth-century specialized ministry and professional practice.

Context: Care and Counseling in American Religious Life

In *A History of Pastoral Care in America*, Brooks Holifield charted the genealogical heritage of twentieth-century pastoral care and counseling. His analysis describes pastoral counseling as a ministry specialty that emerged more than three hundred years ago as the American Protestant church focused its mission in pastoral care. This was part of a larger interactive sociopolitical story that included changes in American culture and economy, changes in how the church and ministers were seen in society, profound advances in medicine and psychology, and theologians' efforts to interpret these shifts and integrate them into a vision for American religious life. Holifield notes that American pastors

> brought to their tasks conflicting traditions, clashing temperaments, disparate methods of "pastoral conversation," and differing views of theology. Indeed, to trace the changing styles of "pastoral care" in America is to tell a story of transformations in theology, psychology, and society.... If one listens throughout a period of three centuries, one can trace a massive shift in clerical

consciousness—a transition from salvation to self-fulfillment—which reveals some of the forces that helped to ensure "the triumph of the therapeutic" in American culture.[7]

In practice, this meant that the central focus of care in the church shifted from concern with salvation and church membership to personal counseling. Rapid evolution of psychological and clinical sciences was central to this changing vision of the central needs of the human person. While theology and ministry had always interacted with the psychologies of their day, Holifield sees America as a special case. American religious thought coalesced around introspective piety that required pastors to know something of parishioners' inner world. This influence was powerful enough for him to claim that "America became a nation of psychologists in part because it had once been a land of Pietists."[8] This basic relationship between religion and psychology, nurtured by the trajectory of American social and political life over three centuries, created a context from which pastoral counseling emerged as a Protestant ministry specialty.

Holifield's text is a foundational document for chaplains and pastoral counselors. I strongly encourage pastoral counselors to read the complete text. My purpose here is to summarize central dimensions of his historical account and to develop several themes that help us understand how pastoral counseling became a specialized practice.

Care in Early American History

Early American pastoral care reflected social and theological issues of the time. Though approaches to care were embedded in four separate Christian traditions—Catholic, Lutheran, Anglican, and Reformed—all were anchored one way or another in helping parishioners manage sin in their internal life. The purpose of care was to foster spiritual growth. Pastors were expected to be expert on inner experience, equipped to help people become sensitive to sin, and able to map personal progress toward religious growth. How pastors understood this was firmly grounded in the American intellectual context. Seventeenth-century pastoral manuals showed a dynamic interplay between pastoral activity, changing social conditions, and innovations in American theology, philosophy, psychology, and ethics. The result was not so much a systematic theology of care as it was a "complex of inherited ideas and images subject to continued modification in changing social and intellectual settings."[9] Care during this period reflected the hierarchies of a colonial social order, most clearly seen in a theological dichotomy between body and soul. People experienced problems in living because they defied established order, especially supernatural authority. This was an internal problem since defiance expressed failure of "higher" mental and spiritual functions to control "lower" dimensions of physicality. Pastoral care most often was wise counsel to support an internal life of obedience. One grew spiritually by learning to subject bodily life to the rule of the spirit, and by obeying God, the highest of all authorities.

The Great Awakening of the mid-1700s added complexity to this hierarchical notion. In the light of revivalism, "Old Light" and "New Light" religious leaders debated how emotion and rationality should be balanced in spiritual growth. New Light revivalists called for primacy of emotional experience while Old Light pastors challenged the effectiveness or appropriateness of emotion unbridled from reason. This struggle pressed disagreeing pastoral theologians such as Charles Chauncy, Jonathan Edwards, and Gilbert Tennent[10] to examine philosophical, psychological, and theological interpretations of human affect and rationality in religious experience. Holifield points to Jonathan Edwards as a master of integration who turned to critical analysis to evaluate the concerns about human will and motivation raised by revivalism. Edwards used John Locke's psychology to raise important theological questions about the human person and to revise Puritan understanding of internal religious life. The result was a forceful, theologically and psychologically balanced position on human volition, emotion, and behavior that helped stabilize care in a revivalist context. This integration was given life by the fact that Edwards also provided a practical model for care. He frequently invited troubled persons, some of whom traveled great distances to consult with him, into his study for conversation and encouraged other pastors to be "easy of access...compassionate, tender and gentle."[11]

The Great Awakening raised significant questions in American religious life. How should rationality and sentiment be managed in the internal life of the soul? How did right behavior and belief relate to feelings and convictions? These questions "popularized a psychological vocabulary and hence a way of thinking about society, politics, and piety. It was that vocabulary and that way of thinking that would shape the cure of souls in America for half a century."[12] This focus inspired pastoral theologians to observe the struggles of spiritual growth, consider classification systems of spiritual maturity, and develop guides for pastoral listening. Counseling consisted of firm advice giving (most often related to effective moral living), finding the religious source of true happiness, and preventing parishioners from pursuing wrong ways of living.

Nineteenth-century life in America shifted away from agrarian roots and toward urbanization, privatization, industrialization, and social segmentation. By midcentury, economic life began to organize loosely around hierarchies of owner and laborer. Factory and merchant trade replaced the home as the center of economic production. Work and family—now separate spheres—organized around more sharply defined gender roles. Men worked away from home in private industry while women guarded the private domestic retreat insulated from the concerns of economic production.[13] Religious life paralleled social developments. The second Great Awakening solidified the priority of evangelical Protestantism in American towns and cities and normalized religious life as voluntary and private. Theologians began to encourage privatization and segmentation.[14]

By the mid-1800s the church's role in American life had changed. Churches, particularly in towns and cities, were no longer primary representatives of a community's identity or arbiters of social values. Instead, they became private communities consisting of volunteers. Pastoral emphasis turned from defining community values and controlling congregants' beliefs and behavior and toward fostering voluntary personal conversion and nurturing individual spiritual life. Clergy became shepherds of a private congregation that could, like a private business, grow and prosper or fail and die. On the one hand, this change signaled a significant loss of ministers' central role in a community. On the other hand, ministry gained status as a career endowed with advancement possibilities similar to vocations in private industry. Pastors were expected to "speak the truth," but also knew that if volunteer congregants were offended, they could leave one congregation for another. Church became a private sphere with congregational life focused on devotionalism and personal experience. According to Holifield, privatization was also stimulated by turmoil over the abolition of slavery. This conflict "prompted many Protestant congregations to define themselves as 'sanctuaries,' centers of devotion secure from the outside world."[15] As social and religious life segregated, pastors turned their attention almost exclusively toward parishioners' inner lives. *Pastoral* now stood in contrast to *public*. These influences marked a transition to what Holifield calls a religious culture of the self. This new religious culture required pastors to experiment with new forms of care and stimulated intense pastoral interest in the psychologies of the nineteenth century.

Holifield offers Ichabod Spencer as a prototype pastoral innovator. Conscious of his diminished pastoral authority, Spencer published *A Pastor's Sketches*[16] in 1850, which modeled a new form of pastoral intervention. Spencer was well acquainted with the psychologists and mental philosophers important to nineteenth-century education in ministry (Francis Bacon, John Locke, David Hume, Thomas Upham, and Dugald Stewart). They offered few methods for counseling, but provided a broad vision of the inner world of the human mind. By understanding internal states, emotions, and motivation, a pastor could help parishioners make the sentimental conscious and reach deeper levels of self-understanding. If care focused on self-knowledge, it could open a pathway for parishioners to act on pastoral advice and carry out important duties. Together self-knowledge and ethical action would produce a harmony of intellect, volition, and sentiment. Spencer advocated "pastoral conversation" as a way to encourage self-knowledge and to guide "anxious enquirers" in the problems of daily life while also sustaining their connection to a worshiping faith community. Spencer's case studies show that he gave specific attention to parishioners' feelings and "sentiments" as a central organizing factor for his pastoral counseling. Though controversial, his method was influential.

As the culture of self gained strength in the late nineteenth century, congregations expected their pastors to provide individual counseling about moral matters and to lead church-based small groups focused on expression of feeling and honest conversation about difficult matters. Pastors needed to be students of human nature and psychology who could classify persons and their problems and guide individuals toward a healthy, balanced sense of self and salvation. Pastoral counseling in this period focused on individual self-control, piety, obedience, and personal watchfulness. Counseling helped parishioners realize self-fulfillment and achieve the internal balance and harmony of a maturing Christian. This was best done by helping church members develop conscience, form character, balance emotion and rationality, experience religious conviction, exhibit good moral behavior, and find ways to move beyond despair. A few pastoral leaders advocated for a new discipline of clinical theology based in the case methods of law and medicine.[17]

Gerkin notes that by the end of the nineteenth century two changes had transformed pastoral care and counseling. First, the congregational context of care had shifted because of volunteerism and privatization. Churches, once primarily a center for worship and evangelism, became the center of social life. Congregations built parlors, as well as space for concerts, children's activities, and other important community events. Social life, including counseling resources for one's emotional and psychological life, could now be centered in a voluntary, private community. Second, the style of pastoral presence in counseling had shifted from direct moral instruction to quiet conversations with parishioners. This "natural" style reflected psychologists' discovery of the unconscious mind and liberal theologians' focus on God's immanent presence in nature. These two shifts supported a culture of self-mastery and prepared the way for what Gerkin calls "the full-blown appropriation of the rapidly developing psychological sciences."[18]

Twentieth-century Context

By the early twentieth century, pastors were less concerned about helping parishioners balance emotion and rationality and more concerned about subconscious dynamics influencing men's and women's feelings and behavior. This was coupled with a liberal Protestant doctrine of divine immanence that supported fundamental trust in the creative action of nature. It was important, therefore, to understand human psychology, especially as it applied to helping parishioners organize their internal life and daily behavior. This matched a dramatic expansion in academic and therapeutic psychology between 1880 and 1910. These disciplines were asking many of the same questions posed by ministers and pastoral theologians struggling with concerns of sin, spiritual growth, and care: What is the nature of human activity? Are there motivations that are unconscious in human life? What difference does unconscious or subconscious motivation make in understanding the human mind? Is conscious activity more important than unconscious activity? What is the nature of human will? What is the relationship between human feeling, thought, and volition? What is the relationship between thought and action? How do these factors influence mental and behavioral healing? How can human religious life be understood psychologically? Several significant developments helped form pastoral counseling as a mid-twentieth-century specialty.

Psychology and Psychotherapy. Prior to the twentieth century, psychological thought informing ministry came primarily from philosophers of the mind. Most academic psychologists were busy trying to establish a hard science, conducting studies to describe states of consciousness, levels of attention, or perception. Few were concerned about therapeutic application that would help clergy understand the interplay between reason and emotion or human problems in living. However, in the late 1890s, William James at Harvard University pushed academic psychology toward more clinical concerns. Psychology, he believed, offered little if what it discovered had no application to improving real human life. James proposed a functionalist[19] psychology to bridge scientific study of the brain and clinical need. He believed it was useless to study structures of the mind in isolation. Sensation and mental experience must be understood in the context in which they occurred. Mind and body were a psychophysical unity. Psychology, he believed, must attend to how the mind adapts to changing physical circumstances as well as to states of mind. This shift provided a way to apply psychology to the concerns of everyday human life and problems.

James's approach had much to offer clergy counselors. Functional psychology made room for the idea that human perception and thought could be organized by will. Furthermore, his vision of an integrated mind and body resolved much of the split between rationality and sentimentality that had dominated nearly a century of pastoral theology. Linking mental activity and behavior provided a pathway for self-fulfillment—an idea that quickly appealed to clergy counselors. For example, in 1892 James defined *habit* as a reciprocal exchange between neurological activity and behavior. That is, the mind stimulated a tendency toward action, but action also influenced the activities of the mind.[20] Habits could be developed systematically or controlled because individuals could decide where to direct their attention. In these decisions, they partially create their environments and their destinies. James's concept of the "willing self" supported counseling that encouraged character development through self-mastery and self-control. These themes made sense in the masculine ethos of pastoral counselors, and pastoral intervention turned toward increased attention to action and self-control.

In his later work, James set the stage for increased pastoral attention to more passive approaches to counseling by emphasizing a "subliminal self" that was not accessible to active, conscious awareness. James refined these ideas in *The Varieties of Religious Experience* where he proposed that religious experience was embedded in individuals' wider experience of self. Saving transformation was grounded in subconscious processes that were beyond the control of conscious action and effort. Religious behavior itself could be "healthy-minded" or "sick-minded" depending upon the underlying internal processes from which it emerged. "Sick souls" would find relief from their internal struggle not through effort but through surrender to internal life. The demands of institutional religion could act to enhance or encumber internal transformation.

The new psychology of religion developed by James, Edwin Starbuck, and James Leuba suggested that religious transformation was not so much an effect received from a transcendent God, but an expression of resources embedded in human psychological structure. Transforming experience, they suggested, lives not in doctrine but in the psychological function of human feelings. This position fit well with liberal Protestant thought emphasizing the authority of personal experience and God's immanent presence in human life. Salvation was a human process. Internal experience was trustworthy, and receptivity to one's personal, inward experience was a pathway to know God.[21] Problems of the soul were not a matter of right belief or doctrine, so answers could not be found in the intellect alone. Pastoral counseling in liberal congregations began to shift away from cognitive, intellectual answers and toward helping parishioners surrender to a "wider self" that would lead to transformation.

James's idea of balance between action and receptivity, the influence of nineteenth-century New Thought,[22] and an emerging psychology of religion expanded Protestant notions of a "natural" approach to counseling. At the same time, neurology was shaping psychotherapy as a "natural" cure for sick souls. By 1910 a growing number of American neurologists and psychologists were drawn to Freud's theory of an unconscious level of mind where infantile forces drove conscious thought and behavior. Psychoanalysis gave therapists of the soul an attractive, complex alternative for understanding behavior and motivation. Though academic psychologists largely rejected Freud's thought, William James predicted that his ideas would soon dominate American psychology and psychotherapy. For pastoral counselors and theologians, psychoanalysis raised awareness that human emotional, spiritual, and volitional life was more complex and mysterious than supposed by earlier theological anthropologies. This implied that effective clergy counseling would require specialized training in the methods of psychotherapy.

The Emmanuel Movement. Advances in psychotherapy quickly attracted the attention of counseling clergy. As early as 1905, parish clergy incorporated psychotherapy as a central part of pastoral care. Emmanuel Church (Episcopal) in Boston provided a model for psychotherapeutic care. Believing that all pastors offered psychotherapy whether they meant to or not, Rector Elwood Worcester pressed for parish care to be guided by science rather than tradition. He led the church to sponsor lectures about therapy and psychological disorders, collaborate with physicians to conduct diagnostic sessions at the church, and form treatment teams to cure "nervous diseases resulting from defects of character."[23] Physicians would make diagnoses and refer appropriate cases for pastoral intervention to church-centered therapists. This new approach quickly spread to well-to-do Protestant congregations throughout the United States and found expression in Europe, Asia, and Africa. Though never developed into a consistent model for therapy, the Emmanuel model exhibited features of James's attention to relaxation and receptivity, Freud's concept of the unconscious, and an expectation that therapy outcome would produce stronger character and moral control.

By the early 1920s, conflict between physicians and clergy began to erode the movement. Physicians initially welcomed clergy as partners in treatment, expecting them to work under the direction of physicians and to limit their work to moral education or suggestive therapy. However, leaders of the Emmanuel movement wanted to build a pastoral psychotherapy that included work with the unconscious to help build character. Physician critics responded that pastoral counselors were confusing theology with therapy and making a substandard attempt to become psychotherapists without medical training. Though short-lived (1905–29), this movement marked the first effort by Protestant clergy to claim treatment authority over psychological problems, address the scientific materialism of early twentieth-century medicine, and offer a model of care that integrated a nonreductionistic vision of body, mind, and spirit.[24]

The Social Gospel and Christian Education. The decade following World War I was what Holifield called a "psychological revival" that left no American institution untouched. This psychological revival was influenced by American soldiers returning from war who had received psychological services in the military, a shift toward the Social Gospel in Protestant thought, and popular fascination with Freud. Psychology, it seemed, promised success through self-realization to a culture that was quickly becoming urban, white collar, and middle class. Popular psychology shifted its focus from character building to developing personalities able to adapt to industry and work well with others. Ministers were expected to offer care informed by these psychological trends. In a 1934 study of ministry education, Mark May found that nearly 80 percent of Protestant clergy had regular private consultations with congregants about personal problems. These ministers also felt unprepared by seminaries to manage these consultations. May concluded that individual counseling was likely to become a permanent and critically important dimension of ministry in the future.[25] Harry Emerson Fosdick, pastor of Riverside Church in New York (1926–1946), argued that the success of the Social Gospel[26] required better-adjusted individuals. He claimed pastoral counseling as the center of his ministry and insisted that the best preaching was personal counseling at a group level. Fosdick's outspoken advocacy for counseling became a model for pastors who were moved by psychology but were skeptical of the psychology of success; "who were eager to learn from Freud but disinclined to pronounce him savior."[27]

Pastoral counseling entered seminary curricula through religious education departments in the 1920s and 1930s. Religious educators were attracted to John Dewey's claim that education was a form of personal growth in which experience was reorganized to inform future action. Dewey's influence was apparent at Union Theological Seminary where George Albert Coe, professor of religious education, taught that religious education should promote individual self-realization. Coe's psychological approach to religious experience and change, and his insistence that care of souls should be organized on definite methods based in knowledge and attention to developmental psychology, formed the basic curriculum in seminaries for pastoral counseling as a specialty. Pastoral counselors studied psychology of religion, developmental psychology, and the increasingly popular theories of Sigmund Freud, Alfred Adler, and Carl Jung. Seminary-trained pastoral counselors found homes in congregations where they became resident psychologists carrying on some of the tradition of the failed Emmanuel movement. Carl Rogers, a leading humanist psychologist of the twentieth century who had a profound later influence on pastoral counseling, credits his education in religious education at Union Seminary with teaching him the value of working with individuals in a helping relationship.

Clinical Pastoral Education. Charles Gerkin[28] described the 1920s as a profoundly transitional time for pastoral care. The Emmanuel movement and Social Gospel movement had begun to wane. The brutality of war and oppression of the early twentieth century led neo-orthodox theologians—particularly Barth—to challenge liberalism's optimism and idealism and to focus on human sinfulness and the need for salvation.[29] During this time a small group of parish ministers organized to offer clinical training in hospitals and social agencies. The group was led by Congregational pastor Anton Boisen. His personal struggle with psychosis led him to two conclusions: that there was a fundamental connection between religious conversion and mental anguish, and that the church had failed in its response to those who suffered with mental illness. As a result, he turned his ministry toward exploring the link between theology and mental suffering and finding ways to minister to those in mental anguish. In 1925 clinical pastoral education was born as Boisen and Boston neurologist Richard Cabot began training a small group of theological students using medical case study methods. Their agenda was partly to transform the Protestant ministry by engaging ministers in concrete episodes of human conflict and pain. This innovation had a profound impact on later pastoral counseling by developing new methods of clinical training and shaping how counselors would appropriate psychotherapeutic theory. New pastoral counseling centers at Wellesley Hills Congregational Church and Old South Church in Boston in the early 1930s gave concrete expression to these ministry innovations. In 1937 the American Foundation of Religion and Psychiatry (AFRP) was established by psychoanalytic psychiatrist Smiley Blanton and author Norman Vincent Peale at the Marble Collegiate Church in New York City. The AFRP's success in training counselors and providing psychotherapy in a religious context helped anchor later efforts to develop a professional guild for pastoral counselors and establish pastoral counselors' institutional identity.

In the mid-1930s Cabot and Boisen parted ways over disagreement about the nature of mental illness. Cabot maintained a strict physical, organic view of mental illness while Boisen focused on psychological factors. Two traditions of clinical training emerged. The Boston group, led by Cabot and Russell Dicks, was grounded in an organic metaphor focused on physical illness, growth, and stability. Their model of counseling[30] assumed that the healing power of God was present in each person's life. The counselor's task was to listen and help individuals find the "growing edge" of their lives presented by their current problem. As counselees discovered God's immanent presence, counselors could help sick and troubled people face and assimilate God's plan for their lives.

Cabot and Dicks's ideas became enduring images that shaped Protestant pastoral counseling for most of the twentieth century. Their model of training emphasized the clergy counselor's persistence, effort, and personal discipline that resulted in competence.

Boisen's focus on psychiatry and pastoral care took root in the New York tradition of clinical training. He believed that psychiatrically troubled people were "living human documents" that provided insight into the human personality. Psychiatric patients' internal lives pointed to a theological vision of a human self characterized by turmoil, struggle, and irrational chaos rather than the positive, divine immanence images of growth proposed by Cabot and Dicks. This turbulent image of human personality drew clinical supervisors toward psychoanalysis and a treatment ethic that valued liberation from internal chaos through insight. Rather than focus on discipline and competence, clinical training in this tradition introduced pastoral counselors to deeper motivations of the self experienced in disorder, conflict, and guilt. Insight into one's own pathological motivation modeled on psychoanalysis became the focus of both clinical training and counseling practice. Rollo May's 1939 book, *The Art of Counseling*, provided a firm platform for this position in pastoral counseling. May, a minister trained at Alfred Adler's Vienna clinic, was a strong advocate of clergy counselors. The task of pastoral counseling, he insisted, was to promote insight through psychological interpretation and theological clarification. Good counseling, though, was not a learned technique. Instead, the active ingredient in counseling is the person of the counselor. Citing Adler and Freud, May asserted that personal analysis was necessary to be an effective therapist.[31] Alongside these clinical developments, Paul Tillich and H. Richard and Reinhold Niebuhr developed theologies in dialogue with psychoanalysis that reinforced the value of insight over earlier concerns with adjustment in pastoral counseling.

Through the 1940s and 1950s, clinical pastoral training quickly spread in seminaries, hospitals, and prisons throughout the United States. In 1967 the two training groups reunited and were joined by Southern Baptist[32] and Lutheran supervisors to form the Association for Clinical Pastoral Education. The association standardized Clinical Pastoral Education (CPE) as a professional education program for ministry that provided supervised practice in pastoral care with a focus on pastoral identity, interpersonal competence, and chaplaincy skills. By the 1950s, pastoral theologians and clinicians were drawing clear distinctions between *pastoral care* and *pastoral counseling*. Pastoral care in its broadest sense was seen as an attitude engendered in faith communities to nurture individuals, families, and the community as a whole in times of need or distress. Care could include preaching, teaching, administration, and community development. More specialized pastoral care, often expressed by chaplains, required specific training to help individuals and families find appropriate emotional support, manage concrete life tasks, and provide religious guidance in times of need. Pastoral counseling was targeted to individual problems (later to include family problems) and looked primarily to psychotherapy as an intervention for care.

Pastoral Counseling: A Clinical Ministry Specialty

The clinical pastoral training movement set the stage for pastoral counseling to develop as a ministry specialty in at least five ways. First, it solidified a frame of reference for ministry specialists to focus on mental health needs. Second, it provided clinically trained leaders who would stimulate pastoral counseling specialization. Third, it consolidated an interdisciplinary medical, psychological, and theological context in which practical ministry could test and integrate counseling methods. This context provided a theological and practical foundation for ministers to borrow psychotherapeutic theories and implement them as integrated forms of ministry. Boisen's legacy insisted that this was not an intellectual task. Integration took place through the personal formation of the minister offering care and not through learning techniques. Those who would help troubled souls as chaplains, counselors, or informed parish ministers must claim identities formed from insight into their own disorders, chaos, and motivations. Psychoanalysis and depth psychologies were most consonant with this vision of the human person and so quickly became favored theories of both clinical pastoral education and early pastoral counseling. This notion of personal, internal transformation as a vehicle of training, integration, and clinical practice was historically powerful. Research eighty years later[33] shows that certified pastoral counselors in the twenty-first century almost universally claim that pastoral counseling is not a learned skill or a theory of therapy. Instead it is an identity. It is "who I am" formed through clinical training. Skills, theories, and actions result from an internal sense of consistency more than a rational, conceptual base. This stands in sharp contrast to alternative models such as the Christian Counseling movement's agenda to establish an intellectual and research discipline of Christian psychology and biblical counselors' insistence that Scripture alone is sufficient for guidance.

Fourth, clinical education defined ministry to troubled souls in a way that bridged congregational life and other contexts of health care. This made room for counseling as a ministry unconstrained by congregational boundaries or traditional tasks of parish ministers.

Fifth, the clinical pastoral education movement advocated for basic clinical education as part of Protestant seminary education. Ministers exposed to clinical training in seminary were more likely than their predecessors to interpret parishioners' problems as mental health issues needing intervention rather than sin or disobedience. Because of clinical training, these pastors understood that intervention in complex religious-mental health problems required substantial skill beyond the training of most congregational pastors. This understanding motivated many to seek further psychotherapeutic training or to refer to clergy counselors who had been trained psychotherapeutically. Both responses encouraged pastoral counseling as a specialty.

Rich interactions between clinical ministry, psychiatry, and psychology in the late 1930s and 1940s sparked an explosion of pastoral counseling centers, training programs, and literature interpreting the relationship between psychotherapy, theology, and ministry. Holifield viewed this as part of a multilayered post–World War II environment that included "a theological revolt against legalism, the recovery of older Protestant doctrines [through neo-orthodoxy's critique of liberalism], a white-collar economy, a burgeoning cultural preoccupation with psychology, postwar affluence, ... a critique of mass culture, and an ethic of self realization."[34] Sociologist and cultural critic Philip Rieff noted that by mid-twentieth century, "I believe" had been replaced by "I feel," which anticipated psychotherapy as the secular spiritual guide of the future.[35] Robert Bellah and his colleagues identified this shift leading to a "culture of the therapeutic" that was focused on individualized happiness. Popular psychology highlighted an ethical responsibility to "find one's self."[36] In growing numbers, postwar Americans turned to counseling and popular psychology to manage life and achieve success. Popular psychology literature had religious overtones and often appeared a more accessible faith than Christianity. Norman Vincent Peale, for instance, believed that his techniques to master mental life were a form of applied Christianity that would ensure health and success.

With therapeutic thought so close to the heart of American culture, it is no surprise that increasing numbers of ministers were drawn to pastoral counseling. Many former military chaplains believed their war experience uniquely qualified them for a special ministry and were drawn toward seminary and pastoral counselor training. Postwar America was prosperous enough to pay them. It is also no surprise that pastoral theologians criticized the culture of the therapeutic. Several called for a more critical and thoughtful integration of psychotherapy into religious life. Pastoral theologian Seward Hiltner acknowledged that popular techniques might offer some temporary relief but contended that they impeded genuine growth. Wayne Oates criticized popular psychology as a cult of reassurance that failed to address internal human contradictions and relegated religion to a personal resource for selfish benefits.[37] Pastoral counselor training responded to popular interest in psychotherapy, but was tempered by the promise that *pastoral* counseling would offer theological and psychotherapeutic depth that transcended temporary relief or a cult of reassurance.

Pastoral counseling specialization gained credibility partly through academic interest in seminaries and graduate schools. Prior to 1940, few seminaries offered counseling courses. By the 1950s, pastoral counselor training was a separate area of seminary training with a unique curriculum. Several universities, including the University of Chicago and Boston University, developed advanced degree programs in personality and theology, pastoral psychology, pastoral theology, and pastoral counseling.

Holifield points to four seminal pastoral theologians who helped define this emerging specialty. Seward Hiltner, a Presbyterian minister and student of Anton Boisen, was professor of pastoral theology at University of Chicago and Princeton Theological Seminary.

His *Pastoral Counseling* (1949) served as a primary text for pastoral counselors through the 1950s. It provided a theoretical foundation for pastoral practice grounded in Hiltner's psychodynamic experience and the emerging work of Carl Rogers. His *Preface to Pastoral Theology* (1958) was the first comprehensive effort to articulate a method by which reflection on pastoral care and counseling acts could inform theology. Carroll Wise, also a student of Boisen, was professor of pastoral psychology and counseling at Garrett Biblical Institute. Wise, influenced by personalist theology,[38] taught that pastoral care and counseling were fundamentally relational. The accepting, caring relationship developed in counseling worked to communicate the "inner meaning of the Gospel" at the point of counselees' human need. His writing[39] illustrated a thorough commitment to Freudian analytic psychology, Rogerian methods of counseling, and psychotherapy as pastoral intervention. Paul Johnson, professor of psychology and pastoral counseling at Boston University, integrated the work of neo-Freudian Harry Stack Sullivan with personalist theology. Like Hiltner and Wise, Johnson relied heavily on the counseling methods of Carl Rogers. Wayne Oates, professor of pastoral care and psychology at Southern Baptist Theological Seminary, provided a conservative, evangelical vision of pastoral counseling that was less reliant on psychoanalysis and Rogerian counseling methods. Instead, he focused on the pastoral counselor as the representative of Christ's care for persons in need of God's saving grace. By defining pastoral counseling in theological terms—as action that affirmed the lordship of Christ, personal dialogue between Creator and creature, the priesthood of all believers, and the power of the Spirit[40]—he was able to integrate new information from social and behavioral sciences into more conservative patterns of clergy counseling.

This was also a decade of rich interaction between theology, psychology, and pastoral practice. Theologian David Roberts suggested that theology and psychotherapy were correlative. Psychotherapy could not do its job without a Christian view, and insights from psychotherapy could deepen theology.[41] In Paul Tillich's theology, pastoral counselors found a method to balance this tension between theology and psychotherapy. Tillich made a distinction between pathological anxiety grounded in neuroses and unresolved human conflicts, and existential anxiety related to human finitude and separation from the ground of being. Psychotherapy could help resolve the conflicts of pathological anxiety, while relief from existential anxiety was found only in acceptance "by that which infinitely transcends one's individual self."[42] Tillich also maintained close personal associations with psychoanalytic therapists in New York. He critically engaged emerging American psychoanalytic theorists and pastoral counselors as they were defining their new specialty. Howard Stone notes that Paul Tillich is referenced by pastoral counseling literature nearly twice as often as any other twentieth-century theologian.[43]

By the mid-1950s, pastoral counseling was defined by two primary characteristics that would dominate its practice and theory for the next fifty years. First, pastoral counseling claimed a model of ministry that was increasingly segregated from general parish ministry. Early pastoral counselors had been trained as psychotherapists in medical and social service contexts. Many believed the most appropriate place for counseling was a clinic or center separated from broader congregational life. More than eighty-five Protestant counseling centers were established between 1950 and 1959. This segregation was motivated in part by a second characteristic defined by Howard Stone:[44] pastoral counselors relied heavily on psychodynamic personality theories and long-term models of therapy that were inaccessible to most parish pastors. According to Stone, this influence was powerful enough to define pastoral counseling for the next half century.

The psychodynamic theories of Harry Stack Sullivan, Karen Horney, and Erich Fromm emphasized an ethic of self-realization through therapy that broke free of social convention, moralism, and authoritarian control. One could not love others, claimed Fromm, if one could not love one's self. Psychotherapy aimed to uncover and release "who we really are." These ideas found consonance with contemporary theology. Bultmann claimed that only by being truly free to be one's self could one be open to an unknown future in God. Bonhoeffer resisted legalism and moralism. Karl Barth pronounced the death of legalism in favor of human freedom to respond to God's grace. Paul Tillich claimed that the human moral imperative was to live into one's essential nature as a free and integrated individual. Self-realization was required in order to obey the command of love. Pastoral theologians saw possibilities in long-term psychotherapy that could plumb the depths of the unconscious and free individuals for growth into new life. Seward Hiltner claimed that psychotherapy resembled forgiveness by helping sinful clients confront, objectify, and transcend their internal law-conscience. This would make room to manage more rational and important ethical concerns. Carroll Wise and Paul Johnson interpreted psychotherapy as an arena of near absolute acceptance. The purpose of counseling was not to change behavior or values, but to form a relationship that valued the person and expressed acceptance and understanding. Holifield notes that this theological and psychotherapeutic constellation of distrust of moralism, rejection of authoritarian institutions, and focus on individual growth and conscience prepared the way for Carl Rogers's profound influence on pastoral counseling.

In his review of fifty years of pastoral literature, Howard Stone[45] observed that "pastoral counseling clearly owes a debt to Freud and those closely associated with him; but the influence of Carl Rogers is greater than that of Freud or any other psychotherapeutic theorist or theologian. . . . The heavy reliance of an entire field on the thinking of one person—Carl Rogers—is astonishing." Rogers began his study of counseling with religious educators at Union Seminary and completed his doctorate in educational psychology at Columbia University. He was deeply influenced by liberal Protestant ideas that the authority for individual action and belief was internal. The human person, according to Rogers, was motivated by an inherent tendency to move toward growth and enhancement, or self-actualization. Instead of focusing on resolving conflicts, therapy was a way to gain insight into one's inner life. Insight would uncover an individual's innate "drive to health" and overcome "subception" of self created by authoritarian parents and damaging institutions. Counselors must be nondirective and empathic, and offer clients "unconditional positive regard." Therapy helped clients "own" their experience and find acceptance for their perceptions, values, and goals. Self-knowledge and self-acceptance moved clients toward self-actualization and new decisions for living. Good therapists must know and accept themselves. This allowed them to be "genuine" by maintaining "congruence" with their own internal life as they empathically connected with their clients.[46]

A number of pastoral theologians and counselors were skeptical of Rogers's absolute emphasis on self-realization and inherent human goodness (particularly those influenced by Boisen and neo-orthodox or evangelical theologies) and continued to use psycho-analytic theories to understand personality development and problems in living.[47] However, by the mid-1950s nondirective Rogerian counseling methods (if not his theory of personality) had become the basic approach of pastoral counseling training and practice. Pastoral theologian Don Browning drew parallels between Rogerian therapy and God's action in atonement,[48] while popular pastoral writers saw Rogers's nondirective style as an embodiment of what good priests and ministers had always done. For instance, Carroll Wise believed that counseling communicated the gospel at the point of human need not through words but through a relationship where deep feelings found expression and acceptance.

Rogers's nondirective approach fit well with the commitments and theological anthropologies of a quickly growing discipline. Furthermore, training in Rogerian methods was manageable in seminary and pastoral counselor training centers. Nondirective methods could be taught in a short period of time, were relatively safe for pastors with little counseling training, and would provide a foundation upon which pastoral counseling specialists could build. It is no surprise that Rogers was one of the first recipients of AAPC's Distinguished Contribution Award. Recent research shows that a half century later pastoral counseling continues to be dominated by reflective, nondirective models of intervention and psychodynamic personality theory.[49]

Development of a Profession

By 1960 psychotherapy was rapidly expanding beyond Freudian psychoanalysis and Rogers's client-centered therapy. Pastoral counselors found options in Frederick Perls's Gestalt Therapy, Viktor Frankl's Logotherapy, a variety of humanistic and existen-tial approaches, and emerging object relations theory. Proliferation of psychotherapy models was matched by training options that fre-quently invited pastoral counselors to train alongside other mental health professionals. Pastoral counselor identity began to shift from clergy who offered psychologically informed counseling to minister-*psychotherapists* informed by theology and processes of pastoral care. By the early 1960s voices within the pastoral counseling movement were calling for a professional guild to affirm the identity of an emerging specialty, to support pastoral counseling in nonparish contexts, and to set professional standards for the field. This call set the stage for the formation of the American Association of Pastoral Counselors.

In 1963, leaders of the American Foundation of Religion and Psychiatry in New York, by then the largest multidisciplinary church counseling center in the country, initiated a conference of one hundred pastoral counselors. The meeting was led by Frederick Kuether, AFRP training director, financed by a New York insurance magnate, and restricted to pastoral counselors "who were actually doing pastoral counseling in a self-aware and publicly announced center."[50] Professors from theological schools were not invited. Denominational representatives and colleagues from allied psychotherapeutic professions were invited as observers only. The meeting highlighted pastoral counseling's rapid growth as a national phenomenon—there were now 149 pastoral counseling centers in 29 states. More than half of them were founded after 1960. Conference speakers stressed the need for a national organization to set standards for counseling centers and to regulate the growth of pastoral counseling as a clergy specialty. A primary agenda was to found a new guild, the American Association of Pastoral Counselors (AAPC). Kuether argued that pastoral counseling did not belong exclusively to the church. He marked a firm boundary between pastoral care and pastoral counseling. The former was to bring people closer to the church and sustain an institution. The latter was not a church activity, but was oriented toward the inner lives of individuals. Pastoral counseling was religious only to the extent that it helped people manage religious aspects of personal problems. Kuether believed that to limit pastoral counseling to the institutional church was to deny its deepest meaning.[51] Howard Clinebell, the first president of AAPC,[52] extended this argument. Pastoral counseling was distinct because of who the counselor was and what the counselor did in therapy apart from any institutional connection with the church. Counselors were "pastoral" by virtue of their theological training, their clergy standing, their use of religious symbols in their work, and their emphasis on spiritual growth in therapy.[53]

The new guild defined pastoral counseling as a specialty centered and regulated outside of parish life. Pastoral counselors were primarily, though not exclusively, located in counseling clinics and private practice apart from the center of the church's worship and social life. Their primary responsibility was to the psychological needs of individuals and only secondarily to the broader mission of the institutional church. Standards of practice and training were removed from denominations and seminary curricula and placed in a regulating agency (AAPC). This stand met with sharp criticism from Seward Hiltner and Wayne Oates, both excluded from the New York meeting because they were seminary professors. Both opposed the new guild. Hiltner vigorously resisted segregating pastoral counseling from parish life. He believed pastoral counseling must stay anchored in the institutional church, and he rejected Clinebell's location of pastoral in the therapeutic person. By definition, *pastoral* was more. The term itself presupposed the symbols of the church and firm connections with parish life. Furthermore, the new guild would encourage ministers to become psychologists and psychiatrists disguised by the mantle of ordination. It would also encourage private practice. Private *pastoral* practice, asserted Hiltner, was a contradiction in terms.[54] Wayne Oates contended that private practice of pastoral counseling was "a violation of the basic character of the ministry and very likely unethical."[55] Neither Hiltner nor Oates joined the new organization, and both continued to focus on pastoral counseling in the context of the larger ministry of the church.[56] Hiltner eventually separated himself from the pastoral counseling movement. Oates joined AAPC in 1969.

Despite sharp criticism from Hiltner and Oates, the newly formed organization gained national attention and grew. The *New York Times* reported the outcome of the founding meeting. A *Newsweek* story (May 6, 1963) titled "Minister as Therapist" suggested pastoral counselors were needed to assist overburdened psychologists and psychiatrists. The article quoted the president of the National Psychological Association for Psychoanalysis as saying that the need was so great for psychotherapists that he welcomed "anyone with training."

Between 1963 and 1964 AAPC was given structural shape through an intensive committee process led by Howard Clinebell. Tension immediately arose around membership standards. Standards defined identity: Who would be in? Who would be out? Where do pastoral counselors work? What do they do? What is their relationship to the church? Central to these questions was a fundamental conflict about how clinical or pastoral members should be. The first set of standards proposed that pastoral counselors have doctoral degrees and training similar to psychoanalysts with near exclusion of pastoral concerns. Clinebell and others envisioned broader standards that avoided a "mental health clinical" model but that would guarantee basic clinical competence and an intentional relationship with the church. They hoped to avoid creating an elite, restrictive membership. After much conversation and debate through a series of position papers, charter members of AAPC in 1964 defined pastoral counselors as "clergymen who do counseling as part of their parish ministry and . . . those clergymen who have acquired specialized training and experience and have become identified as specialists" (1964 Preamble, AAPC Constitution). The membership also approved standards and governance procedures that emphasized pastoral identity, connection with the institutional church, and a foundational base of clinical competence. Van Wagner speculates that this compromise was in part due to the fact that most charter members of AAPC could not meet the highly restrictive standards originally proposed. Tension between pastoral and clinical was built into governance: the Parish Division set standards for counselors in parish contexts, while the Clinical Division set standards for counselors in nonparish contexts. This distinction was eliminated in 1969 in favor of clinical membership with hierarchical categories—Pastoral Counselor in Training, Member, Fellow, and Diplomate. Congregational ministers without extensive clinical training were set aside as nonvoting Pastoral Affiliates.

Though AAPC members were firmly committed to institutionalizing pastoral counseling as a clinical specialty, governance was designed to maintain church relationships. The organization was incorporated as a religiously based group that held a nonprofit religious tax status. Pastoral counselors were by definition ordained ministers. Early leaders worked with the National Council of

Churches and denominations to define a religious endorsement process to anchor the ecclesiastical identity of pastoral counselors who were increasingly detached from parish and denominational life. To be a pastoral counselor, one had to be set aside for that specialized ministry by one's own denomination. This kept pastoral counselors accountable for ministry in their home denominations and allowed AAPC to set clinical standards.

Tension between clinical and pastoral continued to be a central dialogue from 1965 through 1985. Could pastoral counselors be in private practice like other mental health professionals? How should pastoral counselors relate to other professionals? How should ecclesiastically endorsed pastoral counselors relate to increasing emphasis on licenses in mental health practice? One set of voices, led by Wayne Oates, opposed fee-for-service, private pastoral counseling. The practice would erode pastoral identity by making it indistinguishable from other kinds of counseling. AAPC resolved this dispute by issuing standards that defined *pastoral* as a quality of the person providing therapy rather than an ecclesial context or method of payment. Private practice was allowable so long as pastoral counselors maintained a clear pastoral identity and some ecclesial accountability.

In the 1970s legislative pressure was building in the United States to regulate mental health practice. Again, clinical-pastoral tension arose. Should pastoral counselors seek licenses as clinical mental health professionals or claim exemption because of their ministerial standing? This question was resolved on the pastoral side by a 1974 AAPC resolution that pastoral counselors, as clergy and religious leaders, were exempt from licensing laws and would "neither seek nor accept certification or licensure by the state."[57] These same issues would arise again in the 1990s. Remarkably absent from these early formative debates was any substantial question about appropriate models of psychotherapy for pastoral counseling. Psychodynamic and Rogerian approaches were the default position of the guild, which probably reflected strong commitment to these theories in existing training programs. Theological questions apart from pastoral identity were equally absent. Van Wagner suggests early leaders agreed to "let theological issues lie"[58] in favor of establishing an organization.

This priority on clinical focus was not appreciated in the larger culture. Cultural observers Sprecht and Courtney noted with concern that pastoral counseling had abandoned its willingness to challenge individuals' value systems as pastoral counselors "have come to look and act more and more like psychotherapists, just as psychotherapists have come to look and act more and more like priests."[59] Social analyst Barbara Dafoe Whitehead concluded that pastoral counselors' commitment to contemporary psychotherapeutic methods undercut their ability to confront clients' value systems theologically. Fear that theological challenge would damage individual selfhood or be interpreted as moralistic, pastoral counseling ceded moral decision making to the authority of psychotherapy. Whitehead suggests that this had a profound influence on pastoral views of marriage and marital counseling. Pastoral counselors traded the wisdom of religious teachings for a psychological "canon" that had very little evidence of success in marital counseling. She contends that this shift was a significant factor in (1) the escalation of divorce in the 1960s and 1970s; and (2) marital counseling's move from the domain of the church to civil society.[60]

Between 1970 and 1990 the field of pastoral counseling grew and consolidated as a ministry specialty. Pastoral theologian and AAPC Diplomate Larry Graham observed that pastoral counseling had begun as a loosely organized movement led by charismatic leaders with a vision. However, by the end of the 1980s, he saw that it "no longer constitutes merely a movement or emphasis within ministry, but is on the verge of becoming institutionally autonomous"[61] with its own executive leadership, financial bases, standards for membership and practice, socially accepted service and training centers, and standardized ideological orthodoxies. Pastoral counseling was shifting away from clear connections with the church and toward autonomous existence. This autonomy, he claimed, would give pastoral counselors more authority for their own ministry and allow them to rethink their ministry in relationship to church and society.

By 1988, there were nearly three thousand AAPC members who provided an estimated 1.5 million hours of counseling per year, producing approximately fifty-one million dollars in fees. Many of these counselors worked in the one hundred plus pastoral counseling centers established throughout the country. Pastoral counselor training was also well integrated into seminary and graduate school curricula. Most Protestant seminaries had professors of pastoral counseling. Several offered PhD, DMin, or Doctor of Pastoral Counseling (DPC) degrees. Increases in institutional power and autonomy were also evident in how pastoral counseling services were delivered. Corporate business models, like those offered by the Samaritan Institute,[62] were gaining priority over centers based on parish models. James Ewing, former executive director of AAPC, saw standardization of pastoral counseling and the rapid growth of autonomous pastoral counseling centers as forming "a new religious institution."[63] According to Ewing, this new institution had four expressions: (1) the shaman expressed by charismatic private practitioners; (2) congregational pastoral counseling centers; (3) free-standing centers operating variously as referral services for several congregations, social agencies, or corporate health-care providers; and (4) pastoral counselors integrated into larger health-care systems.

One effect of institutionalization was that pastoral counseling had become culturally normalized. It was no longer counter-cultural but was an integrated part of what Robert Bellah called the culture of the therapeutic.[64] Graham suggests that this demonstrates the impact of institutionalized pastoral counseling on a culture. At the same time, this integration requires careful theological reflection to assess how current practices "fracture the communal web of life."[65] Graham hoped that pastoral counseling independent of ecclesiastical structures would reflect not only on how encounters with human pain help shape the theology of the church—the historic task of pastoral theology—but also on how pastoral counselors bring new life to other communities. Pastoral counseling could help revitalize ecclesiology, partly by adding new ethics of personal and social liberation to what it means to be the people of God at work in the world.[66] In this way it could reclaim some of its countercultural history.

Twentieth-century Retrospective

Pastoral counseling has deep roots in Judeo-Christian history. It emerged as a twentieth-century specialty among North American Protestant clergy who incorporated new psychological information into their ministries. By midcentury it was a ministry specialty requiring distinctive training. As a movement, pastoral counseling mirrored Euro-American, middle-class, mainline Protestant cultural priorities. By the late twentieth century it was institutionalized with a clear set of expectations reflecting particular theological, psychotherapeutic, ecclesiological, and organizational ideologies codified into standards of accreditation and practice. As expressed by these standards, pastoral counselors were identified at least partly by the following values:

- A professional identity anchored in clinical psychotherapeutic training supported by theological education
- Professional certification as a pastoral counselor
- A clerical model of ministry that placed pastoral identity in the personal life of the clinician rather than in ecclesial connection and allowed pastoral counselors to function as autonomous psychotherapists
- Institutional autonomy
- Theologies favoring individual growth and long-term therapy
- Models of administration built on American corporate examples
- Models of service that reflected clinical medicine
- Pastoral counseling as an external support and critic to the church
- Counseling segregated from the central social and worship life of the church

Notes

1. Howard Clinebell, "Pastoral Counseling Movement," in *Dictionary of Pastoral Care and Counseling,* ed. Rodney Hunter (Nashville: Abingdon Press, 1990), 857–58.

2. Charles V. Gerkin, *An Introduction to Pastoral Care* (Nashville: Abingdon Press, 1997), 23.

3. John T. McNeill, *A History of the Cure of Souls* (New York: Harper & Row, 1977).

4. William A. Clebsch and Charles R. Jaekle, *Pastoral Care in Historical Perspective* (New York: Harper & Row, 1967), 4.

5. Clebsch and Jaekle conceive of care primarily as an individual, intrapsychic enterprise. This individual focus reflects the interpretive tradition grounding their

historical analysis. Their work is clearly guided by a modern, Cartesian under-standing of the human person not yet informed by developments in general sys-tems theory, feminist critique of individualism, postmodern critique of the Cartesian self, or contemporary theological anthropology that understands the human self as fundamentally socially located. Their insistence that pastoral care ends when it departs from the primary interest of one individual fails to account for fundamental social networks in which people live, are formed, and are sus-tained. It also fails to appreciate the mutual and recursive social nature of prob-lems in living.

6. Gerkin, *An Introduction to Pastoral Care*, 36.

7. E. Brooks Holifield, *A History of Pastoral Care in America: From Salvation to Self-Realization* (Nashville: Abingdon Press, 1983), 16.

8. Ibid., 65.

9. Ibid., 30.

10. For representative examples, see Charles Chauncy, *The New Creature* (Boston, 1741); Charles Chauncy, *Seasonable Thoughts on the State of Religion in New England* (Boston, 1743); Jonathan Edwards, *A Treatise Concerning Religious Affections* (1746), ed. John E. Smith (New Haven, Conn.: Yale University Press, 1959); Gilbert Tennent, *A Persuasive to the Right Use of the Passions in Religion* (Philadelphia, 1760).

11. Jonathan Edwards, *The Great Concern of a Watchman for Souls* (Boston, 1743).

12. Holifield, *A History of Pastoral Care in America*, 106.

13. Tamara K. Hareven, "Themes in the Historical Development of the Family," in *Review of Child Development Research*, vol. 7, The Family, ed. R. D. Parke (Chicago: University of Chicago Press, 1984).

14. Friedrich D. E. Schleiermacher, *On Religion: Speeches to Its Cultured Despisers* (New York: Harper Torchbooks, 1958).

15. Holifield, *A History of Pastoral Care in America*, 125.

16. Ichabod Spencer, *A Pastor's Sketches*, 1st series ed. (New York: 1851; first printing 1850).

17. E. Brooks Holifield, *The Gentlemen Theologians: American Theology in Southern Culture, 1795–1860* (Durham, N.C.: Duke University Press, 1978).

18. Gerkin, *An Introduction to Pastoral Care*, 49.

19. James's functional approach was a departure from the predominant struc-turalist approach of the day. Structuralists, such as Edward Titchener, focused on the *content* of the mind and asserted that all mental experience could be under-stood by examining combinations of simple elements or events within the mind. Functionalists, such as William James, John Dewey, G. Stanley Hall, and James Baldwin, rejected this simple view in favor of understanding the mind in its func-tional context—what it does and how it acts in particular contexts.

20. William James, Psychology: Briefer Course (New York, 1892).

21. Holifield, *A History of Pastoral Care in America*.

22. New Thought was a controversial movement in the late nineteenth century usually credited to Phineas Parkhurst Quimby. It suggested that success and health could be gained by learning techniques of self- abandonment through men-tal discipline. Based on Christian teachings and nineteenth-century metaphysical traditions, it emphasized spirituality, mystical experience, and the power of the

mind over the body. In addition to influencing many Protestant clergy, the movement is credited with inspiring Emanuel Swedenborg, Mary Baker Eddy, Ralph Waldo Emerson, and Franz Mesmer. See Charles S. Braden, *Spirits in Rebellion: The Rise and Development of New Thought* (Dallas: Southern Methodist University, 1963).

23. Holifield, *A History of Pastoral Care in America,* 206.

24. Katherine McCarthy, "Psychotherapy and Religion: The Emmanuel Movement," *Journal of Religion and Health* 23, no. 2 (1984).

25. Mark A. May, "The Education of American Ministers," in *The Profession of the Ministry* (New York: Institute of Social and Religious Research, 1934).

26. The Social Gospel was a late nineteenth- and early twentieth-century liberal movement in American churches that emphasized application of Christian principles to the problems of urbanization and industrialization. Leading figures, such as Washington Gladden and Walter Rauschenbusch, defocused personal, individual sin and emphasized the social nature of sin. Those embracing the Social Gospel believed that society could progress and realize at least some of the kingdom of God. The movement was characterized by idealistic optimism about the future of humanity and by pragmatic, action-oriented intervention in society. Charles Sheldon's 1897 book, *In His Steps,* highlights one Social Gospel position— American society would be dramatically transformed if people's public and private actions were guided by the question, "What would Jesus do?"

27. Holifield, *A History of Pastoral Care in America,* 221.

28. Gerkin, *An Introduction to Pastoral Care.*

29. Sigmund Freud's thought was also deeply affected by these same issues. Freud observed that his primary explanation of human motivation, the pleasure principle, could not explain the brutality of war or cultural oppression. He subsequently revised his theory to include new structures of the mind and a thanatos drive.

30. Richard Cabot and Russell Dicks, *The Art of Ministering to the Sick* (New York: Macmillan, 1936).

31. Rollo May, *The Art of Counseling* (Nashville: Abingdon Press, 1939/1967).

32. See Russell Moore's 2005 essay "Counseling and the Authority of Christ: A New Vision for Biblical Counseling at Southern Baptist Theological Seminary" (Louisville: Southern Baptist Theological Seminary, 2005). Russell Moore, Dean of Southern Baptist Theological Seminary, cites Wayne Oates's introduction of clinical training and pastoral counseling into seminary curricula and Southern Baptist congregational life as a primary contribution to the seminary's and denomination's drift into liberalism. He interprets changes in Southern Seminary's administration, curriculum, and faculty between 1996 and 2006 as intended to correct this drift. This reversed Southern Baptists' participation in clinical training, rejected any form of ministry influenced by behavioral or psychotherapeutic sciences, and asserted that the Bible alone is sufficient for instruction in all matters of human life and problems in living.

33. Loren L. Townsend, "Theological Reflection and the Formation of Pastoral Counselors," in *The Formation of Pastoral Counselors: Challenges and Opportunities,* eds. Duane Bidwell and Joretta Marshall (Binghamton, N.Y.: Haworth Pastoral Press, 2006).

34. Holifield, *A History of Pastoral Care in America: From Salvation to Self-Realization*, 260.

35. Philip Rieff, *The Triumph of the Therapeutic: Uses of Faith after Freud* (Chicago: University of Chicago Press, 1966/1987). Note that Rieff challenged the triumph of the therapeutic: it would undermine individual strength and also challenge democracy.

36. Robert N. Bellah et al., *Habits of the Heart: Individualism and Commitment in American Life* (Berkeley, Calif.: University of California Press, 1985).

37. Seward Hiltner, *Pastoral Counseling* (Nashville: Abingdon Press, 1949).

38. Personalism is a philosophical stand (related to idealism) that highlights the person as the ontological ultimate. This position asserts the priority of mind and spirit; that is, it rejects the idea that the human person is subordinate to any universal Mind or Spirit and any form of psychology that confuses the "true person" with "personality" that is "learned or socially motivated." This philosophical stand is central to humanistic theorists like Rogers, Allport, Maslow, and Perls. Pastoral counseling was especially influenced by personalist theology developed at Boston University, which emphasized the personal nature of God and the unity of all in a Cosmic Person.

39. See Carroll Wise, *The Meaning of Pastoral Care* (New York: Harper & Row, 1966); Carroll Wise, *Pastoral Counseling: Its Theory and Practice* (New York: Harper and Bros., 1951); Carroll Wise, *Pastoral Psychotherapy: Theory and Practice* (Lanham, Md.: Jason Aronson, 1980).

40. Wayne Oates, *Protestant Pastoral Counseling* (Philadelphia: Westminster Press, 1962).

41. David E. Roberts, *Psychotherapy and a Christian View of Man* (New York: Charles Scribner's Sons, 1950).

42. Paul Tillich, *The Courage to Be* (New Haven, Conn.: Yale University Press, 1952), 165.

43. Howard W. Stone, *Strategies for Brief Pastoral Counseling*, ed. Howard W. Stone (Minneapolis: Fortress Press, 2001).

44. Howard Stone, "The Congregational Setting of Pastoral Counseling: A Study of Pastoral Counseling Theorists from 1949–1999," *Journal of Pastoral Care* 55, no. 2 (2001).

45. Ibid., 185.

46. Carl Rogers, *Client-Centered Therapy* (Boston: Houghton Mifflin, 1951); Carl Rogers, *Counseling and Psychotherapy* (Boston: Houghton Mifflin, 1942).

47. Russell Dicks in *Pastoral Work and Personal Counseling* (1949) opposed Rogers by asserting that nondirective counseling did not exist. All counseling was directive in one form or another. This was a criticism of Rogerian methods that resurfaced later in family therapy models of therapy, feminist critique of pastoral counseling, and postmodern expressions of pastoral therapy.

48. Don S. Browning, *Atonement and Psychotherapy* (Philadelphia: Westminster Press, 1966).

49. Howard Stone's (2001) literature review clearly shows this pattern. My own grounded theory study, "What's Pastoral about Pastoral Counseling?" (2005–2007), confirmed this pattern. Qualitative analysis of pastoral statements and interviews of eighty-five certified pastoral counselors selected for maximum

diversity showed homogeneity in choice of personality theory and counseling methods. Almost universally, certified pastoral counselors identified psychodynamic theory as a guide to understanding personality and nondirective, reflective methods of engaging clients. Though only a few counselors named Rogers as a guiding influence, they did report training in programs historically associated with Rogers's influence. Those claiming other positions saw themselves as marginal to the main body of pastoral counselors.

50. Frederick Kuether, as cited in Charles A. Van Wagner, *AAPC in Historical Perspective: 1963–1991*, ed. Allison Stokes (Fairfax, Va.: American Association of Pastoral Counselors, 1991), 4.

51. Frederick Kuether, "Pastoral Counseling: Community or Chaos," *Pastoral Counselor* 1 (1963).

52. At the time of the meeting, Howard Clinebell was director of the Pasadena area Pastoral Counseling Center and Associate Professor at the Southern California School of Theology at Claremont. He was invited to the meeting because of his clinical work and his well-received writing in pastoral counseling. Van Wagner (*AAPC in Historical Perspective*) suggests Clinebell was selected for president because of his relationship with Methodist pastoral counselors at Marble Collegiate Church in New York, his lack of connection with the CPE movement, and his association with Frederick Kuether.

53. Howard Clinebell, "The Challenge of the Specialty of Pastoral Counseling," *Pastoral Psychology* 15 (1964).

54. Seward Hiltner, "The American Association of Pastoral Counselors: A Critique," *Pastoral Psychology* 15 (April 1964).

55. Oates, *Protestant Pastoral Counseling*, 31–32.

56. Van Wagner, *AAPC in Historical Perspective: 1963–1991*, suggests that personal conflicts between Oates and Hiltner and the leaders of the Council for Clinical Training who helped shape AAPC may have been as important as ideological differences in their resistance to the new guild.

57. AAPC Council minutes, April 28, 1974.

58. Van Wagner, *AAPC in Historical Perspective: 1963–1991*, 82.

59. Harry Sprecht and Mark Courtney, *Unfaithful Angels: How Social Work Has Abandoned Its Mission* (New York: Free Press, 1994), 13.

60. Barbara D. Whitehead, *The Divorce Culture: Rethinking Our Commitments to Marriage and Family* (New York: Vintage Books, 1996).

61. Larry Graham, "The Institutionalization of Pastoral Counseling," *Journal of Pastoral Psychotherapy* 1, nos. 3/4 (1988), 7.

62. The Samaritan Institute began in 1972 as a nonprofit organization to promote an interdisciplinary team approach to pastoral counseling. The institute developed a model of management that assisted local religious leaders to build financially successful counseling centers. In 2007, the Samaritan Institute claimed 505 Samaritan Center offices in 364 cities in the United States and Japan (http://www.samaritaninstitute.org/about/index.asp).

63. James W. Ewing, "Theological Implications of the Institutionalization of Pastoral Counseling," *Journal of Pastoral Psychotherapy* 1, nos. 3/4 (1988), 28–29.

64. Bellah et al., *Habits of the Heart: Individualism and Commitment in American Life*.

65. Graham, "The Institutionalization of Pastoral Counseling," 12.

66. Graham cites the work of African American pastoral theologian Archie Smith as particularly promising for this transforming ethic. Smith envisioned an emancipator struggle that helped create free individuals and humane, nonoppressive social structures. Pastoral counseling was about joining the liberating spirit of God who sides with those who are poor and downtrodden by an oppressive society. See Archie Smith Jr., *The Relational Self: Ethics and Therapy from a Black Church Perspective* (Nashville: Abingdon Press, 1982).

CHAPTER 2

Genealogy Revisited: Euro-American Priority

Foundational works in pastoral counseling agree: this ministry emerged as a twentieth-century expression of North American Protestant clergy. These texts also define it as an exclusively Euro-American invention, primarily by rendering non-Euro-American contributions invisible. A case study of African American pastoral counselors provides an instructive example. While other racial and ethnic stories are also obscured by Euro-American priority, African American invisibility is particularly poignant. Black churches have been a strong presence in America for several centuries and have a long-standing tradition of care and counsel. Furthermore, African American ministers have been present from the beginning of the clinical training movement. Yet they are almost invisible in the history of the field. A review of historical texts and data from my own three-year study of pastoral counselors (WPC) highlights this marginalization. My intent here is to describe the shape of a hidden story and suggest a more inclusive genealogy.

Pastoral Counseling Texts

One striking example of African American invisibility is Brooks Holifield's *Pastoral Care in America: From Salvation to Self-Realization*. This is the most comprehensive history of pastoral care

Special thanks to the following colleagues who shared insight and helped interpret data for this chapter: Edward Wimberly, PhD; Homer Ashby, PhD; Alice Graham, PhD; Nancy Long, DMin; Clinton McNair, PhD; Archie Smith Jr., PhD; Lee Butler, PhD; and Vergil Lattimore, PhD.

and counseling to date. It has been a standard for graduate students for a quarter century and provides the historical foundation for nearly every pastoral care book published since 1984. However, Holifield examines pastoral care and counseling *only* as they were expressed by Euro-American leaders, cultural history, and congregational experience. His analysis leads to the inevitable conclusion that pastoral counseling is by historical fact a white, American phenomenon. African Americans are mentioned only as recipients of white religious care and as a concern of abolitionist churches. A single reference to slave-era Black churches noted that care was usually some form of mutual support. In a similar way, AAPC's self-published history[1] remembers no African American or other non-Euro-American contributor to a half century of prehistory, early history, and institutional development of that organization.

A second central text, the *Dictionary of Pastoral Care and Counseling,*[2] has the same pattern. General articles defining the field highlight only Euro-American leaders and contexts. In these articles *church* refers to Euro-American churches. The political processes that produced institutional pastoral counseling are described as white leaders interacting with the academic, medical, and ecclesial institutions they served. There are no references to African American or other non-Euro-American contributors. Contributions by non-Euro-Americans are segregated into articles defined by race or ethnicity (for example, "Black Pastoral Care") and insulated from the larger field-defining general articles. It is striking that the focus of these specialty articles is general pastoral care. This is significant since the *Dictionary* carefully distinguishes between pastoral care and the specialty of pastoral counseling. Structuring the *Dictionary* in this way implies that pastoral counseling does not exist in any independent way in Black religious experience, or that, unlike Euro-American contexts, there is no particular place for counseling specialists in African American contexts. This segregated approach restricts the notion that Black pastoral care or counseling offers any theological or practical contribution to the larger church. The 2005 edition of the *Dictionary* contains a supplement sensitive to issues of race, gender, class, and ethnicity in pastoral care and counseling. It does not, however, include chapters written by African American pastoral theologians, nor does it directly address the segregated history of pastoral counseling.

Howard Stone's analysis of fifty years of pastoral counseling literature (1949–1999)[3] provides another window to observe Euro-American priority. Stone's primary agenda was to demonstrate how pastoral counseling has been professionalized and disconnected from congregational ministry. However, results of this study also highlight the invisibility of non-Euro-American contributions. His content analysis of 46 central and widely read pastoral counseling texts revealed nearly 1,000 references to theologians, none of whom were African American or people of color. Of 449 references to pastoral care or counseling theorists in his sample, a single African American theorist—Archie Smith Jr.—was cited.

Together, these textual examples suggest three implicit but inescapable conclusions:

1. That non-Euro-Americans—specifically African Americans—were absent or had little to offer pastoral counseling's institutionalization and scholarly development;
2. That the African American church has had little to offer as a source of general knowledge for pastoral counseling;
3. That work of Euro-American pastoral theologians and pastoral counselors relates to the field as a whole, but the work of African American pastoral counselors and pastoral theologians is restricted to a kind of "Black project." It is relevant to the African American church and community but not the broader pastoral counseling movement.

In this context, it is no surprise that Edward Wimberly begins his 1979 book, *Pastoral Care in the Black Church*, with a stark but necessary justification: "Pastoral care in the black church has a history. Many persons may have the impression that pastoral care does not exist in the black church because little has been written about it. They may feel that pastoral care is a white-church phenomenon."[4] He goes on to outline patterns of care and counseling in black churches. Although these differ in emphasis from white churches, they express the same healing, sustaining, guiding, and reconciling that have characterized care and counseling through Christian history. He does observe one clear difference. Black church leaders have not had the same economic or political privilege that allowed white church leaders to pursue training and focus on personal healing. Wimberly argues that pastoral counseling and healing ministries will take a more central place as "the black laity becomes better educated and assumes greater leadership in the wider society in the future."[5] He also hopes that exploring care in black churches will highlight "the valuable contribution that the black church has made to pastoral care."[6] In 1982 Vergel Lattimore[7] extended this theme by suggesting that a number of black cultural values made positive contributions to pastoral counseling. He observed that pastoral counseling was captive to white cultural and therapeutic values that embodied racism when they were applied as universal values in counseling. However, pastoral counselors could reduce this captivity, improve work with African American clients, and deepen the discipline's cultural and theoretical foundation by attending to important black cultural values.[8]

In *The Relational Self: Ethics and Therapy from a Black Church Perspective,*[9] Archie Smith Jr. provided a social and theological analysis of oppression and liberation in the context of psychotherapy and African American religious experience. In this groundbreaking work, Smith identified relationality and the communal self as key factors that keep Christian social ethics and pastoral counseling together and guide transforming ministries of liberation. He claimed explicitly that knowledge from African American experience was not segregated knowledge. *The Relational Self* "is written from a black church perspective, but the message is not limited to the black church. The black church is viewed as a microcosm of the Christian church responding to the liberating gospel of Jesus in a racist society."[10]

Wimberly, Lattimore, and Smith are clear. They do not expect care and counseling in the Black church, or their work as African American pastoral counselors and theologians, to be segregated into a racially contained "Black project." Instead, they show how knowledge emerging from Black church experience and African American cultural experience informs and strengthens the whole church and pastoral counseling as a discipline. In his contribution to the *Dictionary of Pastoral Care and Counseling,* theologian Peter Paris argues that "black theology makes a strong stand that soli-

darity with the black American struggle is a fundamental require-
ment of all American Christians desiring to be faithful to Jesus
Christ."[11] Black theology highlights how Euro-American theologies—those most associated with pastoral counseling—uncritically
adopted racist cultural values that pathologized the experience,
culture, motivations, and religious expressions of African
Americans and other oppressed people. This theme echoes
through the history of pastoral counseling as African Americans
were cast as culturally disadvantaged recipients of well-trained
white care[12] and black pastoral counselors were omitted from the
central story of pastoral counseling's institutional history. The aim
of black theology, Paris states, is to engage liberating praxis[13] to
stimulate change in *all* societal structures of racial oppression. This
would include pastoral counseling. This aim rejects the image that
African American communities and churches (and pastoral counselors) are theologically and culturally disadvantaged. Instead, it
highlights African American culture and history as an important
source of indigenous knowledge. It asserts that social transformation to change African American communities and the dominant
Euro-American culture is a theological imperative.

Taking African American scholars and pastoral counselors seriously means refusing to restrict their contributions to defining care
in racial-ethnic communities or helping the pastoral counseling
movement become more cross-culturally competent. Instead,
African American contributions must be integrated into the whole
of the discipline in a way that invites all pastoral counselors to participate in mutual transformation of pastoral identity, clinical practices, and cultural/religious values. Failure to attend to African
American contributions truncates the entire discipline.[14] More personally, pastoral counseling dominated by Euro-American history,
theology, and values forces assimilation. This has a direct effect on
African American pastoral counselors. To gain institutional valida-
tion, pastoral counselors must often accommodate to theories, theologies, and practices that are divorced from or marginally
connected to their history, values, and experience. Such assimilation is a form of racism and oppression. It silences important
voices, represses cultural memory, and ultimately impoverishes
clients and larger society. It also obscures significant information
about oppression, survival, and liberation. As Smith asserts, "The

survival and welfare of black people in this society is inseparable from the survival and well-being of all people."[15] Pastoral counseling is one small microcosm of this observation. The life and welfare of African Americans in pastoral counseling are inseparable from the life and well-being of the field itself.

African American Voices

S. W. is a pastoral counselor who was licensed two years ago. At that time she was recruited to the staff of a suburban counseling center. The director indicated that he was concerned that African American churches in the area were underserved, and her presence would increase the center's ministry to this population. At her first annual evaluation the director affirmed her clinical skills and value to the staff. However, he was disappointed that her caseload had not grown as expected. He was concerned that low production was costing the center and could not justify the first-year increased fee percentage he had promised when she was hired. This would have to wait until she "improved her client recruitment performance."

T. P. has been in private practice for almost twenty years. He has a thriving practice and deeply enjoys his work as a pastoral counselor. He was trained in an AAPC-approved center and identifies himself as a pastoral counselor. However, he is not an AAPC member and does not participate in local, regional, or national pastoral counselor activities. When asked about this, he reported that he withdrew early in his career to maintain emotional health. "Regional leaders would ask my opinion because they wanted 'diversity input.' I would give it. Then I would see a strange look on their face. It wasn't what she—or he—wanted to hear and I never heard from them again. I got tired of being the only quote-unquote 'minority' on committees. More than that, I got tired of having my input ignored."

D. M. is in her final year of training. She appreciates the supervision she received and has a deep sense of loyalty to her training program. However, she fears she will not finish training with the depth of experience gained by her white colleagues. As she entered training, her program had received a grant to provide counseling services to several underserved elementary schools in a predominantly African American community. For "obvious reasons" she was the best choice to manage and provide the services demanded by the grant. Most of her clinical hours were related to this program. Too many of these, she believes, were "babysitting kids the school couldn't manage" and trying to convince parents to take counseling seriously. While she appreciates the administrative experience and the opportunity to be creative, she envies her colleagues who saw "garden variety" clients in the home clinic. She fears she did not get enough experience with middle-class clients, white clients, individual adult issues, and marital issues.

Research interviews (WPC)[16] with African American pastoral counselors revealed a striking consensus that pastoral counseling has been a deeply segregated discipline. This was observed in several ways. First, most respondents believed that early African American leaders were marginalized and forgotten as pastoral counseling found its institutional identity. This confirmed Homer Ashby's observation that "in terms of AAPC membership, leadership in AAPC, teaching on theological faculties, heading pastoral counseling centers, and supervising pastoral counselors... African Americans were like Ralph Ellison's Invisible Man."[17] He and several research respondents identified Thomas Pugh, PhD, as an archetypal example of exclusion and invisibility.

Dr. Pugh is recognized as the first African American to enter pastoral counseling as a developing institution.[18] He was educated at Clark College and Gammon Theological Seminary, and his early ministry with migrant workers and students motivated him toward graduate study to improve his skills. He entered doctoral study at Boston University (one of the few schools in the 1950s willing to admit African Americans)[19] and after one semester changed his focus from New Testament to pastoral counseling. At Boston University he was deeply influenced by Paul Johnson, personalist theology, and the psychology of dynamic interpersonalism. Clinical experience at Massachusetts General Hospital and South Boston community ministries put him in contact with Harry Stack Sullivan, Wayne Oates, Carroll Wise, Grady Davis, and Howard Thurman, and "ushered [him] to the forefront of African-American clergy trained in the latest art of being with people in crisis."[20] As a postdoctoral pastoral counselor and psychologist, Pugh studied psychological testing at the University of Chicago with Samuel Beck, completed a fellowship at the Marriage Council of Philadelphia at the University of Pennsylvania, coauthored scholarly articles with family therapy pioneer Emily Mudd, and completed training at the Menninger Clinic, where Seward Hiltner was on staff. He was a charter member of the American Association of Pastoral Counselors and one of the earliest pastoral counselors to be certified as a marriage and family therapist and approved supervisor. Dr. Pugh was called to the faculty of Interdenominational Theological Center in 1959, where he served until his death in 1994. He designed and taught the center's first courses in pastoral care and counseling, developed the Department of Pastoral Care, and worked for nearly a decade to help African American students gain access to clinical pastoral education in segregated Atlanta. He was one of the few pastoral counselors to pursue and publish empirical research, and his wide interest as a scholar is reflected in a variety of journal articles. His clinical teaching defined an African American pastoral counseling paradigm, which he grounded in personalist theology and dynamic personalism. As an early family therapy supervisor, he helped pastoral counselors integrate the two fields and supervised the first generation of dually certified pastoral counselors in the southeastern United States.

Despite his contributions, Thomas Pugh was not granted the institutional recognition afforded other pioneers. He was never elected to an AAPC office or appointed to a position of leadership. Neither was he granted advanced certification in AAPC or other pastoral counseling organizations. He was posthumously awarded the Distinguished Contribution Award in 2000 when the American Association of Pastoral Counselors met in Atlanta for its annual convention.

Thomas Pugh's career illustrates a history of segregation that appears to have had a lasting impact on African American pastoral counselors. One respondent, certified as a pastoral counselor for more than twenty years, reflected on his own experience and noted, "For some reason ... racism in the pastoral counseling movement was more pronounced than in any other institution at the time." Ed Wimberly clarifies that there seems to be "little transparency or willingness of pastoral counselors to be vulnerable when black folk raise racial issues." This, he concludes, makes pastoral counseling feel like "the last bastion of racism in mainline Protestantism."[21] It is also more than a remote problem of history. Research respondents certified in the early 1980s and those certified twenty-five years later (2002–2005) shared a common perception: becoming a pastoral counselor was an intensely painful and sometimes toxic experience for people of color. Almost all African American pastoral counselors interviewed reported deep ambivalence about their training, careers, and relationships with pastoral counseling institutions. Those educated in primarily African American contexts (such as the Interdenominational Theological Center) reported instances in job and certification interviews where their training was depreciated as limited and applicable primarily to minority populations. Two respondents recalled a deep sense of call to the ministry of pastoral counseling in the early 1980s, but they were discouraged by statements that their heritage in the African American church made them unlikely candidates for pastoral counseling training. Those trained in predominantly white programs reported conflicting demands and expectations. On the one hand, programs communicated appreciation for racial and ethnic difference. On the other hand, African American students were expected to internalize theories normalized within the dominant Euro-American culture and assimilate themselves into practices of pastoral counseling defined by mainline white Protestant clergy. Most indicated that was at the cost of spirituality grounded in Black church experience. They often felt that their cosmology, spiritual expression, and approach to relationships with God and others were incompatible with how psychotherapy was taught and the training program's approach to religious life. Several respondents were clear: they could not be honest about their belief in the spirit world, the place of the ancestral community, or their personal religious expression if they wanted to succeed in pastoral counselor training. Most recalled little or no critical analysis of cultural values expressed by these demands while in training; one respondent recalled a supervisor saying: "Your ethnicity has nothing to do with your clinical work." Respondents discussing these experiences suggested that "getting through training" was difficult for most African Americans, but was especially hard for African American women. Alice Graham noted that it "is often difficult to sustain an awareness of the richness of ethnic heritage in the context of developing clinical skills in an environment whose cultural norms do not affirm and value the differing realities of people of color."[22] Ethnocentric training models and theories of therapy lack sensitivity to the social realities of persons of color and risk "doing violence to the soul."[23]

A number of African American pastoral counselors recalled being pursued by predominantly white training institutions. Most felt their recruitment was expected to benefit the program by adding "color" to the training context, providing "a minority point of view" for other trainees, and acting as a vehicle to attract new nonwhite clients. Almost all respondents trained in those contexts reported episodes of institutional racism in the form of client assignment and progress evaluations. Some recalled being placed in special settings—often segregated from Euro-American trainees—to serve nonwhite clients less able to pay agency fees. Others spoke of bias in client assignment as those responsible for assigning intakes (supervisors or receptionists) were reluctant to assign white clients to African American therapists. They feared the agency would lose money or suffer image problems if clients did not return after being assigned a therapist of color. Several recalled the words "you are not the best match for this client" as code for institutional racism disguised as protection for well-to-do white clients. At times this led to severe training conflicts. Student placement and client assignment procedures made it impossible to maintain an adequate caseload, but students were also negatively evaluated because their client hours and fee production did not match those of white students. Interviews revealed an almost equal measure of appreciation for good supervision and cross-cultural training experiences and cynicism about racial bias in pastoral counseling theory, the demand for assimilation in training,[24] and the effect of tokenism in institutional pastoral counseling.

These same issues followed counselors into professional practice. More than half of the African American pastoral counselors interviewed worked in mainline pastoral counseling clinics. Many reported ongoing problems with client assignment unless there was a large enough African American referral base to fill their caseload. These therapists experienced a familiar tension. They were expected to be well assimilated into dominant Euro-American and mainline Protestant cultural values expressed by their agency, and they were to provide a "minority presence" to meet the needs of ethnic minority, often poor, clients. They were asked to serve less privileged clients but were also judged as less capable of producing income than Euro-American therapists. As in training, these counselors did not believe they could risk honesty about their cosmology or spirituality with their pastoral counseling colleagues. Several pastoral counselors interviewed had resolved these pressures by entering private practice or finding jobs with social service agencies that funded satellite programs in African American communities.

Data revealed one disturbing theme in pastoral counseling that one respondent called a "plantation mentality." In a field dominated by Euro-American mainline Protestant interests, African American pastoral counselors reported feeling valued as clients,[25] students, therapists to underserved populations, and providers of a cross-cultural collegial experience to Euro-Americans. However, most saw little opportunity to express clinical and organizational leadership in established pastoral counseling agencies or to challenge the field's Euro-American status quo. Several examples emerged from interview data. Executive directors and training directors of established pastoral counseling centers have been almost without exception Euro-American. Few African Americans have been recognized as excellent administrators or outstanding supervisors. The primary institutional expression of pastoral counseling in the United States, AAPC, has never elected an African American president or vice president. Several respondents reported serving on AAPC committees, but not without significant frustration. They recalled being the only non-Euro-American committee member and having little power to challenge dominant values: "In a democracy, the majority rules"; "there is never a critical mass of racial diversity on a committee, so nothing changes"; and "I think I was asked to 'add color' to the committee, but not to offer any particular contribution."

In his 2007 plenary address to the American Association of Pastoral Counselors, Archie Smith Jr. appeared to distill the sentiment of many longtime African American pastoral counselors.

Reflecting on his 1988 keynote address to AAPC, Smith recalled being told by pastoral counselors at the time "that what I offered about cultural differences was not relevant and cannot be used by pastoral counselors."[26] He went on to express hope that this sentiment was dated and that we are making progress toward a world that makes religious understanding across cultural difference imperative. Interviews between 2005 and 2007 (WPC) suggest that for African American pastoral counselors, little has changed since 1988.

These historic issues have had consequences. As Homer Ashby stated,

> Institutionalized racism was so dominant and persistent that it was a long time before African Americans became long-lasting members of the movement.... The lingering effect is that younger African Americans interested in the field look at the profession with skepticism and suspicion and some older African Americans . . . have lessened their interest in the pastoral counseling movement.[27]

It is striking that, despite marginalization, tokenism, and institutionalized racism, most African American pastoral counselors interviewed were passionate about their training and work. Students seemed willing to endure racial problems because they believed pastoral counseling was vital to the Black community and they were growing personally. A number of seasoned pastoral counselors expressed hope that the field could still be transformed, and they were willing to work personally and institutionally toward that end. This optimism is enhanced by a growing body of Africentric pastoral theological literature. Examples include Carroll Watkins Ali's[28] indigenous approach to pastoral theology and Homer Ashby's new theological vision for African American community.[29] Lee Butler has constructed an interdisciplinary Theory of African American Communal Identity Formation (TAACIF)[30] that is grounded in cultural analysis, womanist and liberation theologies, African (Black) psychologies, and psychodynamic theories. It offers a forthright corrective to pastoral counseling theories, theologies, and practices that dehumanize African Americans.

Notes

1. Charles A. Van Wagner, *AAPC in Historical Perspective: 1963–1991,* ed. Allison Stokes (Fairfax, Va.: American Association of Pastoral Counselors, 1991).

2. R. Hunter, *Dictionary of Pastoral Care and Counseling* (Nashville: Abingdon Press, 1990).

3. Howard Stone, "The Congregational Setting of Pastoral Counseling: A Study of Pastoral Counseling Theorists from 1949–1999," *Journal of Pastoral Care* 55, no. 2 (2001); Howard W. Stone, *Strategies for Brief Pastoral Counseling,* ed. Howard W. Stone (Minneapolis: Fortress Press, 2001).

4. Edward P. Wimberly, *Pastoral Care in the Black Church* (Nashville: Abingdon Press, 1979), 17–18.

5. Ibid., 123.

6. Ibid., 8.

7. Vergel L. Lattimore III, "The Positive Contribution of Black Cultural Values to Pastoral Counseling," *Journal of Pastoral Care* 36, no. 2 (1982).

8. Values suggested by Lattimore include collective identity, commitment to family life, a work orientation, and improvisation as a lifestyle.

9. Archie Smith Jr., *The Relational Self: Ethics and Therapy from a Black Church Perspective* (Nashville: Abingdon Press, 1982).

10. Ibid., 14.

11. P. J. Paris, "Black Theology and Pastoral Care," in *Dictionary of Pastoral Care and Counseling,* ed. Rodney Hunter (Nashville: Abingdon Press, 1990), 99.

12. For example, Charles Kemp, *Pastoral Care with the Poor* (Nashville: Abingdon Press, 1972).

13. Liberative praxis refers to a method of theological reflection commonly used by liberation theologies. It begins in the experience of oppressed people and turns to multiple theological sources, including social analysis, to construct action toward empowering oppressed communities.

14. In 2008 the AAPC funded a Multicultural Competencies and Racial Justice Project, which has the agenda (1) to enhance the organization's future by addressing an increasingly diverse client population, (2) to move the organization toward anti-racism and racial healing, and (3) to integrate anti-racist attitudes and multicultural practices into the professional formation of AAPC members.

15. Smith, *The Relational Self: Ethics and Therapy from a Black Church Perspective,* 25.

16. As part of "What's Pastoral about Pastoral Counseling?" twenty-eight individuals who met study criteria were identified as African American by AAPC records. The study includes data from eighteen African American respondents.

17. Personal communication, 2007.

18. Editors, "Presenting the Issue," *Journal of Interdenominational Theological Center* 25, no. 3 (1998). Dr. Pugh's personal history is recorded in this same issue of the *Journal.*

19. Wimberly and McCrary state that Boston University's tradition of personalist philosophy assigned human worth without regard to corporeal factors such as race, which "allowed entry to persons who previously had not been accorded

the status of personhood. This move ensured survival of the Personalist Tradition in the African-American Community." Edward P. Wimberly and Carolyn L. McCrary, "Introduction: Personhood in African-American Pastoral Care," *Journal of Interdenominational Theological Center* 25, no. 3 (1998): 27. Boston personalist influence on pastoral counseling is outlined in chapter 1.

20. Ibid., 27.

21. Personal communication, 2008.

22. Alice M. Graham, "Race and Ethnicity in the Formation of Pastoral Counselors," in *The Formation of Pastoral Counselors: Challenges and Opportunities,* eds. Duane Bidwell and Joretta Marshall (Binghamton, N.Y.: Haworth Pastoral Press, 2006), 91.

23. Ibid., 94.

24. Analysis of data suggests a difference in perception between African American pastoral counselors trained in traditional pastoral counseling programs and those trained in nonpastoral counseling university contexts. This latter group gained entrance to the field through what AAPC now calls the Mental Health Track. They are ordained ministers (or theologically trained) and hold a license to counsel in an allied mental health profession but have not completed a traditional sequence of pastoral counselor training in a training center or seminary. These people expressed a sense of marginalization that was not clearly race related. They tended to attribute feeling "out of the loop" to their lack of traditional pastoral counseling training. At the same time they almost universally noted that African Americans are highly underrepresented in the field and in the field's leadership. These counselors were less concerned with historic issues of African American inclusion but were ambivalent about their association with a field so heavily dominated by Euro-American values, methods, participation, and leadership.

25. This appears to be a qualified value. African American respondents recalled good therapy experiences but also recalled a level of marginalization as clients. In many cases, being an African American client meant being seen as poor or culturally deprived, or being a racial underclass in need of special benevolence from the dominant overclass.

26. Archie Smith Jr., "Locating Loss, Resilience, and Hope in God's Mindfulness," in *2007 AAPC National Convention* (Portland, Oreg.: 2007).

27. Personal communication, 2008.

28. Carroll Watkins Ali, *Survival and Liberation: Pastoral Theology in African American Context* (St. Louis: Chalice Press, 1999).

29. Homer U. Ashby Jr., *Our Home Is over Jordan: A Black Pastoral Theology* (St. Louis: Chalice Press, 2003).

30. Lee H. Butler Jr., *Liberating Our Dignity, Saving Our Souls* (St. Louis: Chalice Press, 2006).

CHAPTER 3

Contemporary Pastoral Counseling

In the mid- and late 1990s, cultural and religious shifts changed the landscape that had supported pastoral counseling for a half century. Mainline Protestant denominations struggled with internal conflicts and declining membership. Racial, ethnic, class, gender, international, and sexual diversity began to challenge the practices, theories, and institutional identity of pastoral counselors. States increased their legislative control over all counseling disciplines. Managed care rearranged rules for the way in which mental health and counseling services were delivered and financed. These were serious challenges to pastoral counselors' self-identification and practices. Institutional growth slowed abruptly. Membership in AAPC declined as members left to pursue other careers or join other mental health disciplines. Potential new members opted for non-pastoral counseling professions that guaranteed state licenses and access to managed care panels. A number of accredited training centers closed. Seminary programs long supportive of pastoral counseling shifted away from clinical education.

By the late 1990s it was clear that pastoral counseling, defined as a North American movement among mostly male, Euro-American, clinically trained Protestant clergy, was stretched thin. In *Pastoral Care and Counseling: Redefining the Paradigms*, Nancy Ramsay described dramatic shifts in the field between 1990 and 2004 as a "sea change." Summarizing the book's six collaborative essays, Ramsay concluded that two new paradigms were "gradually eclipsing the Clinical Pastoral Paradigm"[1] that supported pastoral care and counseling for most of the twentieth century. This paradigm relied on ordination to define *pastoral* and on psychodynamic psychotherapy to explain human motivation and society. This emphasis on psychotherapy stimulated clinical specialization in ministry and led pastoral counselors to organize care in individualistic and privatized practice. A Communal Contextual Paradigm emerged in the 1990s as a powerful alternative to the Clinical Pastoral Paradigm. This paradigm shifts focus away from professional clinical practice based in a culture of individualism. In its place is an ecological metaphor that balances "ecclesial contexts that sustain and strengthen community practices of care" with "widening the horizons of the field that conceive of care as including public, structural, and political dimensions of individual and relational experience."[2] This approach does not reject psychotherapeutic practice and theory. It does insist that clinical focus be linked directly to broader public and relational concerns. A second alternative, the Intercultural Paradigm, also draws on an ecological metaphor, but focuses more directly on the place of cultural, racial, and religious pluralism in care. The shift to these new paradigms is far from complete. However, their growing presence challenges the near hegemony of twentieth-century therapeutic models of care,[3] points out how these have obscured other social and ecclesial priorities, upends pastoral counselors' individualistic clinical priority, and requires that pastoral counselors reshape practices for a diverse, multicultural environment.

One of the first diversity issues confronted by institutional pastoral counseling was that of ordination. Standards of the traditional Clinical Pastoral Paradigm restricted pastoral counseling to ordained, denominationally endorsed[4] ministers. Thus, many women and most gay and lesbian people were excluded. In the early 1990s, AAPC was challenged to change policies that required ordination. After several years of intense debate, AAPC amended its bylaws to allow ordination equivalencies. Bylaws retained a normative definition of *pastoral counselor* as an ordained, seminary-educated (and, some contended, predominantly male, heterosexual, and white) minister but allowed exceptions for those who could not be ordained or endorsed by their faith group. This raised questions for religious judicatories and some pastoral counselors. What was pastoral about pastoral counseling if it was delivered by folk who were neither ordained nor endorsed as ministers by their religious traditions?[5] As pastoral counseling lived through the first decade of the twenty-first century, the institutional response to this question was ambivalence—or more positively, creative tension. Though ordination remained the standard, both ordained and nonordained people were accepted for AAPC membership and state certification where that was available.

This tension was reflected in recent (WPC 2005–2007) research results. Pastoral counselors as a group appear deeply ambivalent about what defines pastoral counseling. Their responses recapitulate historical debate about whether pastoral signifies ecclesial connections (Oates, Hiltner) or the counselor's own internalized religious or spiritual position (Wise, Clinebell). Most ordained and endorsed respondents (and Catholic religious women) interviewed regarded pastoral as a function of their location within the church. Pastoral identity was a function of being "set aside" for specialized ministry. On the other hand, nonordained respondents tended to interpret pastoral as a personal attribute—it reflected how they integrated their own spiritual life into the counseling task. Several saw themselves as "spiritual clinicians" rather than pastoral counselors. One respondent, a non-Protestant, nonordained male, described becoming a pastoral counselor as the culmination of his spiritual growth. For him the role of pastoral counselor served as "an alternative priesthood," whose authority rested in psychological training and his commitment to spiritual care. Today it is likely that most pastoral counselors form a pastoral identity somewhere between these two poles. As one Southern Baptist woman stated in her interview: "I'm ordained, but religiously marginalized. I hold close to my heart what Wayne Oates said. The church may or may not give me permission to do ministry, but it is my client who ultimately ordains me."

Questions about pastoral identity were compounded by changes in the broader field of mental health. By anchoring practice in institutional certification, pastoral counselors moved away from moorings in congregational ministry and embraced a model based in therapeutic medicine. By the late 1980s most pastoral counselors worked in specialized counseling centers or private practice. However, health care reorganization in the 1990s fragmented this traditional practice of psychotherapy. Managed care companies controlled which professional a client could see, what kind of counseling a client would receive, and how long counseling would continue. These policies were rarely generous toward pastoral counselors who lacked licenses and a viable political voice. To complicate matters, when pastoral counselors were accepted by managed care, they were often required to use models of therapy inconsistent with most pastoral counselors' long-term approach. Counselors employed by churches or religious organizations were least affected by changes in health care. Those who depended on health insurance and fees for service as mental health providers were most affected.

Managed care and legislative control of counseling through state licenses pressed pastoral counselors to reexamine their identity, training, and clinical practices. Those who were traditionally trained had few options. Three responses emerged.

1. *Congregational counselors.* Some pastoral counselors reaffirmed their clerical identity and reclaimed an older, nonmedical model of care. These counselors became congregational ministers with counseling expertise or worked in creative relationships with several congregations to offer counseling services. Many preached, led worship, and participated in congregational pastoral care in addition to counseling. They were far less reluctant than other pastoral counselors to initiate conversations about faith, pray with clients, self-identify as ministers, and use office space to highlight religious symbols. For these counselors, authority and responsibility for practice rested in their religious commitments focused in ordination, their psychotherapeutic and theological training, and their relationship to their religious tradition. In the study (WPC), congregational counselors maintained historic identities in clerical ministry but also faced several tensions. On the one hand, they articulated the clearest and most unified sense of pastoral identity, religious accountability, and their position in ministry. They did not see themselves as mental health practitioners in competition with psychologists, professional counselors, or marriage and family therapists. Most viewed psychotherapy as an extension of religious care; some regarded counseling as a form of spiritual direction informed by psychotherapy theory. When speaking of their work, they interpreted problems in living as part of a larger tapestry of religious or spiritual wholeness. On the other hand, these counselors tended to have practices limited to a specific religious community, those who could afford to pay for services, and

those who self-identified as needing religious guidance. They also tended toward privatized contexts, rarely seeing pastoral counseling as part of a public discourse about religious life and human wellness.

2. *Legislative activism.* A second response to the health-care crisis redefined pastoral counseling as a mental health discipline and lobbied state legislatures for the same recognition afforded marriage and family therapists, professional counselors, and social workers. More than two decades of work produced pastoral counseling licenses or certificates in six states (New Hampshire, North Carolina, Maine, Kentucky, Tennessee, and Arkansas). While these laws gave pastoral counselors some equity with other mental health disciplines, they were effective only in religiously conservative states with enough pastoral counselors to form an effective lobby. In other states, the legislative process proved expensive, slow, and unpredictable. Furthermore, defining pastoral counseling as a mental health discipline had its own problems. First, many pastoral counselors discovered that a pastoral counseling license or certificate failed to guarantee competitive access to managed care panels dominated by stronger lobby groups. Second, state legislatures defined pastoral counseling by setting educational requirements, framing public identity, and prescribing standards, ethics, and boundaries of practice. Authority and responsibility for ministry shifted from ecclesial bodies to state regulatory boards. This is not a minor point. It recapitulated historic debates about the legitimate location of pastoral counseling. Should pastoral counseling be defined and regulated by the church, or was it a broader field defined by the counselor's professional identity, theological education, and use of religious symbols? Legislative activism clearly opted for the latter. On the one hand, this option expanded the role of pastoral counselors. On the other hand, these counselors faced a substantial task—to make theological sense of pastoral counseling as one *mental health* discipline among others, regulated by non-ecclesial authority, which operated with standards and practices that had little connection to specific religious communities. Nearly twenty years later, there seems to be little progress in clarifying these important theological and social tensions.

Legislative activism was complicated by two additional factors. First, lobbying for licenses was not broadly successful. Although legislation benefited a particular group of pastoral counselors left out of managed care in the 1990s, very few applied for licenses or certificates after the first wave of those who lobbied for recognition. Second, legislative activists were hard-pressed to define a set of skills or practices unique to pastoral counseling. Unlike practitioners of other disciplines, pastoral counselors had not pursued programs of research to define and legitimize its practices. Consequently, pastoral counselors could not argue that their services differed much from those delivered by other disciplines. Neither could they present evidence that pastoral counseling had procedures to treat specific problems. Instead, legislative activism rested on a political argument: states should recognize faith-based counseling as a viable option for religious people. This proved particularly complex since most mental health professions now claim competence in religious issues and spirituality.

3. *Pastoral counseling: a "bridge discipline."* By the turn of the twenty-first century, most pastoral counselors practicing outside congregational settings could not survive without a professional license. In most states, pastoral counselors were not strong enough to lobby for licenses, and many rejected the idea that a state legislature should regulate ministry. Another alternative was to interpret pastoral counseling as a "bridge discipline" that held ministry and the behavioral sciences in creative tension. This position did not rely on clerical identity, a unique clinical-pastoral counseling theory, or clinical practices that set pastoral counselors apart. Instead, it assumed that theories and skills used by pastoral counselors were identical to those of other psychotherapeutic disciplines. All of our theories of human behavior, human systems, behavioral pathology, and approaches to intervention are borrowed from (or at least firmly grounded in) behavioral sciences. Pastoral counseling is unique because it offers a set of theological methods or spiritual reflective practices to hold counseling theories and procedures in critical conversations with various theological and religious partners. This approach gained critical weight as truth claims of theories and theologies upon which pastoral counseling depended were deconstructed by postmodernity, as new models of therapy proliferated and were shown to be as effective as old models, and as evidence mounted that therapeutic theories and techniques accounted for only a small percentage of change in

psychotherapy. As part of a bridge discipline, pastoral counselors were encouraged to be competent, licensed therapists in an "adopted" therapeutic discipline while anchoring their pastoral identities in religious communities, theological methods, and theories of ministry. Pastoral counseling becomes

> the "holding environment" for multiple models of counseling and the interpretive frame for the motion of therapy. It is an informed dialogical position. Pastoral counselors are not united by a common license, but live in collaborative, conversational relationships with groups such as AAPC [and other professional disciplines]. This approach is highly inclusive, allows competitive practice, and affirms that a pastoral approach to therapy is unique.... These changes downplay traditional clinical certification [by AAPC] and invite diverse mental health professionals to join core conversations with pastoral counselors.[6]

Difference and Creativity

The notion of an interpretive bridge discipline is one way to make sense of the diversity stimulated by the decline of the Clinical Pastoral Paradigm and the need to engage racial, ethnic, gender, sexual orientation, and class differences. However, it does require the field to hold together diverse academic degrees, training experience, theories, theologies, religious faiths, licenses and certification, and practice settings in some kind of coherent framework. Rethinking pastoral identity can clarify differences and highlight important factors that hold pastoral counselors together as a field of interest, study, and practice.

Pastoral sets "our" kind of counseling apart from other kinds. The meaning of this adjective varies widely even among clergy counselors trained in traditional AAPC-associated programs.[7] Most often, *pastoral* describes a function of an individual's formation into religious vocation, an idea favored because it expresses pastoral counseling's foundation in Protestant spiritual and religious heritage. Bidwell and Marshall note that pastoral counselors have generally seen this formation as a multifaceted process that includes "elements of self-awareness, faithful spirituality that honors diversity, psychotherapeutic skills and competency, intentionally life-long learning, and an understanding of the history and ethos of the pastoral counseling community."[8] These were embodied in AAPC standards that required advanced theological degrees, study of psychotherapeutic theory, and personal self-awareness gained through personal therapy. However, formation tied so closely to education for ministry fails to reflect contemporary realities.

Bidwell and Marshall broaden AAPC's restrictive definition of formation by excluding specifics of *ministerial* education and identity. For them, pastoral counselor formation is embodied by "life-long, constitutive processes and practices that call forth and shape a person's integrative pastoral identity. Formation creates and clarifies the values, commitments, and habits of the pastoral counselor and gives form to personal, professional and pastoral identity."[9] Personal formation is a concept largely unchanged from previous generations. It describes fostering qualities such as congruity, warmth, empathy, and self-awareness, usually through personal therapy. Professional formation includes an ethos and knowledge base structured by education, training, identity, practice, and experience. According to these authors, what makes this process pastoral is *content*, or the notion that both personal and professional formation are grounded in the faith experience and ecclesial connection of the individual counselor.

This broader definition creates space for a variety of formative narratives capable of constructing pastoral identity in the crucible of the multiple ecclesial, theological, and educational realities that express pastoral counseling in the twenty-first century. Research results (WPC) from a sample of eighty-five pastoral counselors selected for maximum diversity place identity at the center of how pastoral counselors describe their work. "Pastoral is who I am, not what I do" was an almost universal response when counselors were asked what made their work pastoral instead of some other kind of counseling. This was followed by a closely related theme: "What I do is made pastoral by who I am." These assertions were consistent regardless of whether respondents were clergy or non-clergy, Christian or non-Christian, traditionally trained in seminary and a postgraduate internship, or trained in an alternative nontraditional context. When the nuances of these statements were explored, it was clear that identity was a central organizing concept. All therapist behaviors, thoughts, intents, and interactions were pastoral since these *originated in the person of the therapist*. In fact, most pastoral counselors in the sample denied a set of pastoral skills. Instead, pastoral was a form of "being in relationship" with clients and depended upon "formation of the pastoral self." This was described variously as "bringing my spiritual self into the room" with clients, "thinking through a theological lens" about clients, "being God's representative in the session," "asking the big questions about meaning in therapy," or "reflecting theologically on cases." In rare instances *pastoral* referred to skills for intentional religious conversations with clients, praying for or with clients, using religious rituals, or making direct references to religious or spiritual life. African American counselors and counselors from evangelical traditions were more likely to incorporate specifically religious conversations and activities in therapy. Most pastoral counselors sampled believed there was a close relationship between pastoral identity and psychodynamic training, citing a connection between psychoanalysis's focus on individual personality development and historic pastoral-clinical values of self-awareness. Several respondents believed psychoanalytic training and personal therapy were necessary to assure pastoral identity development.

"Pastoral is who I am, not what I do" is a central value for pastoral counselors. However, research data suggest a far more complex and recursive dynamic between "who I am" and "what I do." Identity clearly emerges as a narrative that organizes pastoral counselors' thinking and intervention. However, identity narratives themselves are constructed within a local and context-specific community of pastoral *practice*. This practice, or set of practices, is context specific. They embody a local and specific history, ethos, and a particular constellation of normative expectations relatedto theory, theology, supervision, and organization of professional tasks. By joining a community of practice, prospective pastoral counselors enter a constructive, interactive process that reorganizes the counselor-in-training's psychological system and produces a unique interpretive narrative of identity. This narrative expresses a distinct appropriation of the community's ethos, values, and pastoral sensibilities.[10] This constructive process suggests that pastoral identity is better described as a narrative that expresses the identity/practice matrix of a community of meaning than a personal quality or attribute owned by the counselor.

Understanding pastoral identity as a narrative connected in a mutually informing, dynamic relationship with a community of practice accomplishes several things. First, it clarifies the connection between pastoral identity and a community of practice. "What I do" is not made pastoral because it is an extension of an essential personal quality or personal spiritual commitment ("who I am"). Instead, "who I am" has been formed by "what I do (or did)" in a very particular social context. Community-specific interactions fill an identity narrative with meaning, give authority to the claim of pastoral, and provide a link of relational accountability.

Second, this understanding provides a frame for restraining an overindulged individualism in pastoral counseling. Pastoral does not emerge from an isolated or idiosyncratic "who I am." One's sensibility of what is pastoral is insufficient in isolation from a community of practice and interpretation. Innovation must take place in critical conversation with the community (or communities) of meaning that ground the notion of pastoral.

Third, this understanding allows us to see that local narratives are connected by structural similarities. Data suggest that the "who I am" / "what I do" (identity/practice) matrix is anchored in several factors common to those who identify themselves as pastoral counselors. These cross diverse community boundaries and include intense examination of one's self as a counselor; conscientious religious or spiritual thought about one's profession, clients, and sometimes the context of counseling and therapeutic theory; a desire for religious, spiritual, or theological insight into the therapeutic process; and a conscious sense of bringing one's self as a religious or spiritual resource into the client's world of meaning.

Research conclusions affirm but also temper Bidwell and Marshall's assertion that the *pastoral* dimension of formation is grounded in the content of faith experience and ecclesial connection of the individual counselor. This appears true so long as faith experience and ecclesial connections are fundamental values of the community of meaning in which identity narratives are formed. In fact, research respondents showed wide variation in the content of their pastoral identity. For most clergy pastoral counselors and those trained in traditional contexts (seminary and AAPC training programs), Bidwell and Marshall's assessment appears accurate. For a substantial and quickly growing group of counselors trained in other contexts, *pastoral* was a much broader term. Most often it did reflect personal spiritual experience but frequently did not anchor this to ecclesial connections or a specific faith tradition.

Fourth, the idea of multiple identity narratives formed through local and context-specific communities of practice helps articulate the many ways that communities of counselors define and relate *pastoral* to *counseling*. It makes room for religious diversity, a variety of therapeutic theories, and broad expansion of where pastoral counselors work and how they identify themselves in the church, community, and public life. It also makes space for counselors licensed as marriage and family therapists, social workers, professional counselors, or psychologists to claim pastoral as central to their identity independent of guild certification. However, the idea that pastoral identity may be as diverse as the communities in which narratives found life also creates the potential for misunderstanding and power struggles. To avoid fragmentation of the field, pastoral counselors must develop theories and theologies of difference that allow mutual respect and room for multiversal practices.

Finally, this understanding of identity undermines the notion of a singular or universal pastoral identity that can be defined by the guild (AAPC) or contained within the Clinical Pastoral Paradigm of pastoral counseling. Thinking about multiple pastoral identities holds more promise for the field's future, especially as it continues to diversify and migrate away from institutional identity lodged only in AAPC membership. Tracing changes in how and where pastoral counselors enter the field, how they self-identify, and how and where they work illustrates this diversity. It also highlights the difficulty in drawing clear boundaries between who is and who is not a pastoral counselor, and what is or is not pastoral counseling.

Pathways

Pastoral counselors historically entered the field through a multistaged process that began in seminary and preparation for ordination. CPE served as a clinical foundation, and at least some parish experience was required before moving toward counseling specialization. Induction into the guild of pastoral counselors took place through years of apprenticeship as a Pastoral Counselor in Training. Clinical membership was the last step, based on the counselor's ability to demonstrate competency to an AAPC admissions committee. This pathway provided, and continues to provide, a very clear identity narrative tied closely to ordination and the Clinical Pastoral Paradigm. Except in rare cases this training does not result in state licensure.

Most people pursuing pastoral counseling specialization today do not expect to be ordained. This development has dramatically reduced the appeal of traditional training and has stimulated licensable degree programs designed for nonclergy pastoral counselors. Several seminaries and divinity schools now offer licensable degrees in marriage and family therapy or professional counseling. These meet license standards and provide the formative religious context of a seminary but do not result in ordination. Such programs focus on integrating theology and behavioral sciences with a dual expectation: that theories of ministry will shape the identity and counseling practices of graduates, and that counseling practices will inform theologies and theories of ministry that shape the broader life of the church. This pathway retains a traditional location and context for ministry preparation. It separates pastoral counseling from its historic clerical heritage while connecting it through licensing to a broader public culture.

Some clergy followed a third, and less common, path to pastoral counseling by earning a licensable degree to augment their training in ministry. In these cases minister and counselor appear in identity narratives as two separate realms. Integration of the two was most often a by-product of the pastor's personal creativity rather than formative community interaction around pastoral identity and counseling practices. Most often these counselors did not complete apprenticeship requirements of AAPC and were ineligible for guild membership. Changes in AAPC policy now encourage these pastors to identify as pastoral counselors and participate in formative discourse.

University-based pastoral counseling degrees represent a further step away from a clerical model of pastoral counseling. Loyola University of Maryland provides an excellent example. Pastoral counseling was an option within the university's psychology department as early as 1976. In the intervening years, Pastoral

Counseling and Spiritual Care became a self-contained department that offered both master's and doctoral degrees. Unlike schools offering traditional and seminary specialty programs, Loyola describes pastoral counseling in psychological instead of religious language:

> The Pastoral Counseling Program, holistic in scope, seeks to understand the human person's search for meaning and purpose in all its complexity. The program espouses an eclectic focus utilizing person-centered, cognitive-behavioral, psychodynamic, and family systems approaches. In addition, the program attempts to interpret human behavior and human experience as an integration of the psychological, the intellectual, the emotional, the social and the spiritual.[11]

> Pastoral Counseling is a helping relationship that intentionally incorporates people's openness to religion and spirituality for the purpose of clients flourishing in their emotional and psychological domains.[12]

This approach redefines pastoral counseling as a subspecialty of Professional Counseling. The program is CACREP[13] accredited and prepares students to be Licensed Professional Counselors. Unlike traditional and seminary-based programs, Loyola's makes no specific claim that pastoral counseling is an extension of the church's ministry or that pastoral counseling is tied to students' faith traditions or religious commitments. Instead, pastoral counseling is tied to specific psychological skills, a frame of reference open to spiritual experience in counseling, and the ability to work within a context of spirituality and human search for meaning. Expected outcomes are psychological rather than religious or spiritual—helping clients flourish "in their emotional and psychological domains." Pastoral identity narratives and expectations of practice formed in this context vary substantially from those formed in traditional training or seminary/divinity programs. Perhaps most important, this approach to pastoral counseling has been embraced by a number of religious and state universities and is shaping the future of the field. More pastoral counselors are currently trained in these programs, some now offered online, than in traditional and seminary specialty programs combined.

International expressions of pastoral counseling also enrich our contemporary understanding of the field's diversity. Lartey[14] has described widely varying international, indigenous contexts that shape both identity narratives and practices. These often show the influence of North American clinical-clerical models of counseling since a number of international leaders were trained in the United States. However, regional and local cultural history shapes how pastoral counseling is understood, how counselors are trained, how they identify themselves, and what they do. Lartey points out that when pastoral counseling takes an indigenous form, it embodies a specific cultural heritage and may look quite different from individualistic American approaches. Pastoral counseling in the Asian-Pacific region and Africa provides examples. Asian understanding of one's self in community is central to any counseling practice in that region. Individual counseling must be anchored within concern and care for the entire community. Lartey cites Methodist Bishop Solomon of Singapore's interpretation that pastoral counseling must see whole communities as clients:

> The community itself may need to be seen as the client or patient.... [W]e will have to help communities in the same way we have been helping individuals and families. We may have to think about how communities experience stress, anxiety, grief, loss, identity crisis, and depression, and how they develop, and suffer dysfunction. We will have to study the secret of resilient communities, communal myths, scripts, coping styles, and so on. We will also have to deal with issues of justice and compassion for these are important markers of the health and well being of a community.[15]

In a similar way, pastoral counseling in Africa must be framed within traditional African life and thought. According to Lartey, it is appropriate to speak of an "African cultural milieu that is manifest in assumptions and practices."[16] These have distinctive characteristics. They assume a pervasive, enduring, and central position for religion in life. There is no split between sacred and secular, and a world of unseen forces, spirits, gods, and ancestors has a crucial relationship with humanity and society. The African cultural milieu also assumes that life is holistic and synthetic. All dimensions of life—human, social, and spiritual—are connected. Finally,

Africans live with a communal understanding in which belonging is of more value than individual expression. The African Association for Pastoral Studies and Counseling was formed to promote training from a "distinctly African perspective." In addition to Asian-Pacific and African expressions of pastoral counseling, Lartey describes indigenous regional trajectories for pastoral counseling in the Philippines, Korea, China, India, and Latin America. In each region, and in regions he does not include, pastoral counseling develops with a unique set of culturally specific values, practices, and understanding of the counselor and the human person in community. These shape identity narratives for counselors in these regions and add diversity to the field.

One notable innovation for how counseling becomes pastoral is observed in institutional mission and practices independent of individual pastoral counselors' training or identity. The Samaritan Institute provides an excellent example of how diversity can be engaged institutionally by constructing a corporate identity narrative that transcends individual clerical, religious, theoretical, and disciplinary commitments. The institute was formed in 1972 to provide resources for emerging pastoral counseling centers. It was tied closely to a Clinical Pastoral Paradigm, and its centers were staffed primarily by AAPC-affiliated counselors. However, the same changes driving diversity in the field also challenged Samaritan Centers. In response, the Samaritan Institute shifted its defining language away from any unified vision of pastoral counseling and toward a diverse institutional collaborative providing care.

> Counseling at Samaritan Centers is provided by licensed and/or certified professionals who represent various disciplines, e.g., psychology, clinical social work, marriage and family therapy, pastoral counseling, psychiatry, etc.... Samaritan counseling, however, goes beyond the traditional requirements of secular mental health agencies. Staff counselors have expertise in theology and are attuned to spiritual issues. They are active in their religion and are able to help clients build upon the context of their own faith in the healing process.... The Samaritan Institute's mission is to help affiliated Centers provide team-oriented, cost-efficient counseling, education, and consultation which emphasize the interrelatedness of mind, body, spirit, and community.[17]

While personal identity narratives are not denied, the central focus is an *institutional* identity that defines mission and context. There is no clear distinction between the religiously based, spiritual, or therapeutic services offered by variously trained or licensed practitioners. Pastoral counseling is not set apart as a distinct discipline so much as all professionals together provide a pastoral context in which religious or spiritual care is managed. This collaborative understanding of pastoral holds great promise as a model for the way in which pastoral counselors can manage diversity and maintain pastoral identity. The Samaritan Institute is one of the largest providers of counseling with 500 offices in 365 cities in the United States and Japan.

One casualty of diversity and multiple identity narratives is guild membership. Most pastoral counselors now enter the field in nontraditional ways and do not enter the guild (AAPC) as an institutional expression of their identity. Most find their authority to practice through state licensing and view guild membership as redundant. Membership remains important for clergy pastoral counselors, those whose practice location requires ecclesial connection, and those who desire a clear institutionally verified identity as a pastoral counselor. As guild certification declines in value, redefining it as a forum for collaborative discourse about pastoral counseling in a rapidly expanding context of diversity and as a location for maintaining collegial relationships holds promise.

Conclusion

Social and religious changes have reshaped pastoral counselor training, practices, and identity. Individuals who cannot or do not wish to be ordained, those who do not have a clerical relationship with a faith group, and clergy who are licensed separately in a behavioral science without traditional apprenticeship now have access to the field. Pastoral counselors also have access to professional licenses in cognate fields. New training programs define pastoral counseling as a field of study and practice independent of a particular guild (AAPC). These facts introduce pastoral counselors to rich cross-disciplinary discourse, expand the range of identity narratives, open new vocational doors, and suggest real promise for pastoral counseling as a bridge discipline. Pastoral counseling will be enriched by theories and theologies of difference that can foster full inclusion of marginalized African American contributions into the field's history and value the various voices of gender, race, class, sexual orientation, and faith tradition. Increased conversation across international boundaries promises to expand our vision in ways yet unknown.

Diversity, and the idea that pastoral identity is multiple and context specific, also raises serious, unanswered questions about identity and practice: What does pastoral mean if one is state licensed and working in a public institution apart from ecclesial authority or accountability? How do pastoral practices fit into a secular or interreligious practice context? What are the limits of theological thinking when the public in which we practice extends beyond specific faith communities? How does a more public practice influence new theological information for the church and other religious traditions? What publics can pastoral counseling legitimately serve? How should competing interpretations of such information between diverse groups of pastoral counselors with differing faith and theoretical commitments be managed? These questions, among others, must press pastoral counselors toward an understanding of difference that supports diverse contexts of practice, frames multiversal methods in the field, stimulates critical analysis of pastoral identity in new contexts, and helps multiple expressions of pastoral counseling find useful connections. Such conversations—which are fundamentally theological—will help the field avoid fragmenting into competing factions based on ecclesial connections, practice methods, or definitions of identity.

Despite these risks, pastoral counseling has greater potential to thrive by *increasing* diversity. This will require us to make sense of our identities, connections, theologies, practices, and theories in specific social locations and political environments. In one location pastoral counseling may express the counseling of parish pastors; in another it may express a group of theologically trained or religiously anchored psychologists and social workers collaborating around cases; in yet another it may be expressed by interprofessional dialogue about communities, organizations, management, or relationships between clinicians, church, and client. Individual identities will vary in a similar way: Is a psychologist or marriage and family therapist trained with spiritual competencies a pastoral counselor? Is a Christian counselor or biblical counselor also a pastoral counselor, or a parish pastor counseling with congregation members? Are there Muslim or Hindu pastoral counselors? Defining pastoral counseling as a bridge discipline and pastoral counselor identity as a narrative constructed within a specific community of practice and interpretation would conditionally answer yes to all of the above. A pastoral counselor is a therapist connected in a variety of ways to the diverse history of religious care and counseling, whose therapeutic and personal formation includes narrative-shaping experience in a community of practice; and that community of practice is connected with the larger community of pastoral counselors through shared history, practices, institutional commitments, or logical rationale.

Notes

1. Nancy Ramsay, "A Time of Ferment and Redefinition," in *Pastoral Care and Counseling: Redefining the Paradigms,* ed. Nancy Ramsay (Nashville: Abingdon Press, 2004), 1.

2. Ibid., 1.

3. *Therapeutic* here refers to a metaphor of illness and health as central to human motivation, personality development, and relational systems. Historically, pastoral counselors have relied almost exclusively on theories of personality based in individual psychology to provide a guiding vision of human motivation, behavior, relational interactions, and their disruptions (pathologies). Many contemporary counseling theories do not share these assumptions. This is particularly true for postmodern approaches.

4. Since its inception, AAPC has required that pastoral counselors be endorsed for the specialized ministry of pastoral counseling by their ordaining denomination. Most mainline Protestant, evangelical, and Catholic judicatories developed processes by which pastoral counselors were set aside for and held accountable for specialized ministry.

5. In 2007 debate about alternative endorsement was renewed as various religious judicatories questioned the purpose and use of AAPC endorsing practices that appeared to undermine responsibility to specific faith groups.

6. Loren Townsend, "Ferment and Imagination in Training in Clinical Ministry," in *Pastoral Counseling: Redefining the Paradigm,* ed. Nancy Ramsay (Nashville: Abingdon Press, 2004), 121.

7. Interviews with pastoral counselors reveal a strong correlation between where individuals were trained and their definition of *pastoral*. For instance, interviews suggest that Blanton Peale graduates nuance pastoral toward a function of the counselor's individual internal dynamics as these are expressed in relationship to clients. Graduates of the Virginia Institute of Pastoral Care tended to emphasize pastoral in relationship to the history of pastoral counseling education,

their clerical identity, and their own and clients' relationship to religious communities. See also Loren L. Townsend, "Theological Reflection and the Formation of Pastoral Counselors," in *The Formation of Pastoral Counselors: Challenges and Opportunities*, eds. Duane Bidwell and Joretta Marshall (Binghamton, N.Y.: Haworth Pastoral Press, 2006).

8. Duane Bidwell and Joretta Marshall, eds., *The Formation of Pastoral Counselors: Challenges and Opportunities* (Binghamton, N.Y.: Haworth Pastoral Press, 2006), 2–3.

9. Ibid., 3.

10. For a more complete description of this interactive and contextual process of identity formation, see Townsend, "Theological Reflection and the Formation of Pastoral Counselors," 31.

11. "Mission Statement of the Pastoral Counseling Program," Loyola College in Maryland, http://www.loyola.edu/pastoralcounseling/about/mission (accessed October 16, 2008).

12. J. Ciarrocchi, Pastoral Counseling Program at Loyola College in Maryland, http://www.loyola.edu/pastoralcounseling/index.html (accessed October 16, 2008).

13. Council for Accreditation of Counseling and Related Educational Programs.

14. Emmanuel Lartey, "Globalization, Internationalization, and Indigenization of Pastoral Care and Counseling," in *Pastoral Care and Counseling: Redefining the Paradigms*, ed. Nancy Ramsay (Nashville: Abingdon Press, 2004).

15. Robert Solomon, "The Future Landscape of Pastoral Care and Counseling in the Asia Pacific Region," in *International Perspectives on Pastoral Counseling*, ed. James Farris (Binghamton, N.Y.: Haworth Pastoral Press, 2002), 113.

16. Lartey, "Globalization, Internationalization, and Indigenization of Pastoral Care and Counseling," 100.

17. The Samaritan Institute, http://www.samaritaninstitute.org/about/index.asp (accessed October 16, 2008).

SECTION II

Practices: What Do Pastoral Counselors Do?

CHAPTER 4

Identity and Integrating Behavioral Science and Theology

Pastoral counselors organize their thought and work around pastoral identity; they integrate behavioral sciences and theology. When asked the research question, "What makes the counseling you do pastoral rather than some other kind of counseling?" almost all answered "my identity." Closely following this, often as a second answer to the same question, were responses such as: "I integrate theology and behavioral sciences," or "I hold spirituality and psychotherapy together." This meant different things for different people but was almost always central to their sense of what made them pastoral. Making sense of behavioral sciences in the light of theology and faith practices has always been close to the heart of pastoral counseling. How pastoral counselors manage that interface defines the field and helps set pastoral counselors apart from biblical counselors and counseling disciplines that make no claim to religious or faith foundations. Chapter 3 highlighted pastoral counselor identity formation as a central organizing factor for the field. Whether this results in an identity grounded in a Clinical Pastoral Paradigm of ordained clergy, a theological bridge discipline paradigm of collaborative diversity, or an interdisciplinary organizational paradigm, this sense of identity anchors what pastoral counselors do. "I integrate psychotherapy and theology" is not easily separated from "pastoral counseling is not what I do; it's who I am."

Most pastoral counselors participating in the study claimed an "integrated" way to "hold theology (or spirituality) and psychotherapy together." Some spoke of this as a "spiritually integrated psychotherapy." When examined, *integrated* usually meant "personally integrated." It referred specifically to an internalized, intuitive sense of appropriate harmony between theology and behavioral sciences (or psychotherapy and spirituality) that was congruent with personal values, assumptions, and faith tradition. Pastoral counselors interviewed were often unable to identify specific procedures or critical analytical processes they used to relate these two sources. Integration was not a procedure, a critical process, or a systematic synthesis of two disciplines but rather something that happened internally. Most pointed to the formative influence of how their training program managed the interface between two or more disciplines. Most thought critical analysis as a form of integration was an important theological concern but did not feel particularly skilled in "thinking through" the interface between behavioral sciences and theology. Most modeled their theological thinking after influential supervisors and restricted it to specific client situations, believing that psychological and religious (or spiritual) meanings would coalesce in counseling practices.

All counselors, pastoral or not, implicitly or explicitly manage the boundary between personal faith, religious or spiritual knowledge, and psychotherapy. Because of their claim to engage the spiritual and religious lives of clients, pastoral counselors must be more intentional about this than other kinds of counselors. This is particularly complex since pastoral counseling is no longer contained as an extension of Protestant ministry or bound historically, philosophically, theologically, or institutionally to the context and practices of the church. These boundaries have been expanded by diversity among pastoral counselors, by the culturally and religiously plural contexts in which they practice, and by a flood of new knowledge from human sciences. Pastoral counselors must engage an increasingly plural world with a versatile, critically examined theological vocabulary that expresses the discipline's voice in relation to the following:

- Intra-Christian counseling contexts that cross boundaries between Protestant, Catholic, Orthodox, conservative evangelical, Holiness, and other traditions;
- Conversations about counseling and human well-being in *inter*religious contexts;

- Public policy and its effect on physical, psychological, and spiritual life as expressed in community mental health and other social service agencies; and
- Public policy affecting human physical, psychological, and spiritual welfare as expressed by legislation and social action.

Dialogue in these larger arenas—and work with expanding diversity of client populations—requires pastoral counselors to be clear about how they manage the boundaries between behavioral sciences and theology, or spirituality and psychotherapy.

Integration does indeed appear to be a function of identity for pastoral counselors. At face value this is an intuitive operation. However, examined more closely, a more concrete picture emerges. Identity itself is a narrative formed in interaction with a specific tradition of pastoral counseling. Embedded in this narrative are assimilated attitudes, assumptions, and procedural instructions that guide the process of integration. Ian Barbour has proposed four philosophical positions that help us sort out how pastoral counselors manage the boundary between behavioral sciences and theology, spirituality and psychotherapy.

Definitions

Several definitions are important to the following discussion:

- *Religion.* For Barbour *religion* refers to a life-guiding philosophical frame of reference expressed by a system of belief and practice lived out in specific cultural contexts. Pastoral counselors tend to use this word in a less precise and more popular way. It refers variously to the religious dimension of individual consciousness, the practices of a particular faith group, or a philosophical system. Often *religion* is used to distinguish a faith community's practices and truth statements from individual spirituality (attitudes, guiding principles, or "orienting-one's-self-in-the-world" practices).
- *Theology.* Barbour uses the term to refer to a system of thought and language that expresses the religious experience and truth of a particular religious community. Theology gives interpretive form to religion, religious experience, and religious

practice. Pastoral counselors use *theology* variously to speak of a system of interpretive thought, doctrine, or a way of thinking that is specifically religious. This is distinct from spirituality, spiritual practices, or spiritual thought. Spirituality does not necessitate theology, though spiritual experience can inspire theology, and theology can inspire spirituality.

- *Pastoral theology.* This term has a variety of meanings. For the purpose of this book, it refers to the primary theological discipline that informs pastoral counseling. It uses information from pastoral counseling experience to construct new theological meaning by focusing on acts of care, theories, practices, and methods. It uses methods of reflection to deepen theological understanding of human need, healing, and transformation, and to enhance pastoral skill. Pastoral theology takes seriously reciprocal conversations between humans' experience of need, theoretical resources (human and behavioral sciences), faith traditions, and specific situations of care.[1] When pastoral counselors use theological reflection to inform or integrate their work with clients, they are usually employing a method developed by pastoral theologians and accessing theological knowledge constructed by pastoral theologians. Pastoral theology is an important historical and contemporary anchor for Protestant, Catholic, and some evangelical pastoral counselors. It is less so for pastoral counselors claiming other religious traditions.

- *Spiritual and spirituality.* These terms are particularly difficult to define in the context of pastoral counseling. As pastoral counselors use them, they reflect a broad range of popular, political, and religious meaning. Popular definitions refer to the natural human ability to explore the deepest dimensions of the human experience and transcend one's self in service of greater causes, meanings, and realities. In this context, spirituality is seen as independent of specific religious expression. *Spiritual* is also used politically to codify a discrete and observable dimension of human life that transcends biophysical existence. This dimension is available for study, clinical definition, social or clinical intervention, and organization as a resource for living. Religious definitions articulate a specific faith community's vision of how individuals apprehend ultimate concerns (or the presence of God) and how this awareness enlivens belief, religious practice, moral decision making, and movement toward renewed possibilities. At the end of this chapter I will address some complexities of pastoral counselors' claim to integrate spirituality and psychotherapy or practice spiritually integrated psychotherapy.

Four Positions for Relating Behavioral Sciences and Theology

Holding science and religion together is an epistemological problem.[2] Epistemology asks: how do we gain knowledge, and how do we know that what we know is trustworthy? This is a particular problem for science and religion since they approach knowledge differently. Religion relies on tradition, personal experience as interpreted by a community, spiritual practices, and the authority of texts or spiritual leaders. Science relies on hypotheses tested by empirical observation, measurement, experimentation, and consensus of a scientific community. Tension grew between science and religion after the seventeenth-century scientific revolution. By the twentieth century, the scientific paradigm had become the singular source of reliable knowledge in American and Western culture. This was at the expense of religious knowledge grounded in Scripture, tradition, and spiritual practices. Barbour describes four common epistemological positions for managing information from these two sources: Conflict, Independence, Dialogue, and Integration. By examining these, we can clarify how pastoral counselors manage the intersection between behavioral sciences and religion and how they can select appropriate methods for integrating their work in a pluralistic culture. As a matter of convenience, I will consider the conflict position last. It is rarely, if ever, a position taken by pastoral counselors. It is a common position for biblical counselors and part of the public conversation about counseling and faith.

Independence

John P. is a pastoral counselor certified by AAPC. He is an ordained graduate of an evangelical seminary. His ten years of experience as a

military chaplain motivated him to specialize in pastoral counseling. Upon leaving the military, John completed a residency in pastoral counseling at an AAPC training center and a degree in professional counseling at a nearby university. John is part of a group private practice associated with a large evangelical congregation. Brochures for his practice emphasize that he is a Christian counselor who takes his clients' faith concerns seriously and grounds his work in Christian faith. He states that his primary goal is to help Christians live effective lives. The foundation for this is spiritual—that is, Christian doctrine and practices provide a template for fulfilled living. However, people often have problems in living that create pain or keep them from a satisfying personal, marital, or family life. Behavioral sciences help him understand mental illnesses and lifestyle factors that undermine clients' ability to live into Christian fullness. Counseling theories give him specific procedures he can use in session to help clients change. When asked how he makes decisions about information from behavioral sciences, or which counseling methods he uses, John stated that, in the final analysis, they must be consistent with Christian morality and a Christian view of human life. Behavioral sciences, he suggests, can help diagnose behavioral and mental problems; they can provide useful methods for behavioral change. They go too far, he believes, when they suggest moral values or how people should live. He would not accept a counseling theory, for instance, that emphasized "moral relativism" or the outcomes of a behavioral scientific study that produced a vision of individual, marital, or family life contrary to his basic understanding of evangelical Christian values and doctrine.

Mary T. is a licensed psychologist and a member of AAPC. She completed her PhD in clinical psychology from a state university. She is a member of a mainline Protestant church, completed a lay ministry program, and considers her faith values central to her identity. Her first clinical job was with a Samaritan Center, where she became involved with pastoral counseling. The center's publicity identifies her as a psychologist and pastoral counselor who practices "spiritually integrated psychotherapy." When asked how she makes decisions about theory and client care, Mary stated that she is a psychologist. Her assessment and treatment methods are guided by empirical data from that discipline. However, she is convinced that the "spiritual dimension" of people's lives is important to their overall well-being and plays a significant role in their healing. She assesses clients' "spiritual resources" and uses these to augment psycho-

logical interventions. In general she feels no conflict between her practice as a psychologist and her religious commitments. Her psychological training is the authority for her mental health practice. Her faith is the authority for her personal spirituality and value system. As a clinician she will move away from psychology into "the spiritual dimension" when required by client need. She is unconcerned that psychological theories might conflict with theology because "they really say nothing that excludes faith, spirituality, or central Christian doctrines." In a similar way, Christian faith does not provide psychological treatment methods. She is, she states, a Christian and a psychologist, not a Christian psychologist.

These two vignettes are examples of pastoral counselors approaching behavioral sciences and theology from a position of independence. This position assumes that science and religion are entirely independent and autonomous. "Each must tend to its own business and not meddle in the affairs of the other."[3] Both produce their own knowledge without eclipsing the other, first because they represent separate domains, and second because they have different languages, methods, and functions. God's domain is history. Science's domain is nature. Religious language interprets history and meaning; scientific language describes the natural universe. This position allows a faith tradition, like Christianity, to prioritize the Bible as the record of revelatory events without resorting to biblical literalism or the certainties of creation science. It also allows scientists to give priority to their discipline in matters of research and application but to retain faith as a personally organizing foundation.

Barbour notes that neo-orthodox and existential theologies helped define independence as a viable position. The purpose of neo-orthodoxy was to recover the Reformation's emphasis on God's revelation in Christ while also accepting advances in science. For Barth, this meant that God could be known only through God's self-disclosure in Christ. Faith depends entirely on revelation, but the world can be known through science. Theologian Langdon Gilkey, who testified in 1985 against an Arkansas law requiring that creation science be taught on equal ground with evolution,[4] marked several important distinctions between scientific and religious knowledge and language: science explains objective, repeatable, and public data while religion seeks to understand order and beauty and inner human experience; science asks *how* questions about objective observations while religion asks *why* questions about origin, human purpose, and human meaning; science's authority is logical coherence and experiment while religion's final authority is God's revelation; science makes predictions that can be experimentally verified while religion uses symbolic language reflective of a transcendent God.[5] Practical theologian Don Browning suggests the notion of separate domains is important for the relationship between psychology and theology. He points out that when psychology steps beyond discrete, empirical observation and begins to instruct people about how to organize moral life, it transcends science and becomes religion. Religion, on the other hand, provides a foundation for moral life and meaning. It makes no claims of an empirical description of nature or human life.[6] Existentialism helps define the distinction between religion and science by contrasting personal selfhood (which can be known only through subjective exploration) with impersonal objects (which can be known through scientific detachment).

Independence is a position common to pastoral counselors and other psychotherapists. It is a milder form of spirit/material or mind/body dualism than the conflict position described below, and it values both behavioral sciences and religious knowledge. Psychologists, for example, can treat mental health problems while valuing issues of faith as a separate domain, which must be managed in a separate language and perhaps by separate practitioners. Pastoral counselors can value behavioral sciences as a legitimate realm of knowledge about human functioning and counseling procedures, but can also turn to religious or theological authority to "work with the spiritual dimension" of a problem or address religious and moral issues. Independence provides space for correlation (finding common ground between social sciences and religion), though disagreements are usually resolved in favor of religiously revealed truth. Correlation is a method common to neo-orthodoxy, Paul Tillich, pastoral theologians like Wayne Oates, and Christian counselors. It grounds contemporary Christian counselors' attempt to develop a distinctly Christian psychology that will use scientific methods but that will also contain results within the boundaries of evangelical Christian theology.[7]

Research results show that independence is a relatively common position for religiously conservative pastoral counselors, those who work with nonreligious clients, and those who work in public mental health contexts. It is also common among counselors who trained primarily as psychologists, marriage and family therapists, social workers, and professional counselors who augment their work with "spiritual competencies."

Dialogue

Pat M. is a pastoral counselor who completed a pastoral counseling degree in seminary and trained for two years in a postgraduate pastoral counselor training center. She is in private practice and self-defines as a pastoral counselor who is licensed as a professional counselor. Like Mary, she defines what she does as "spiritually integrated psychotherapy." When asked to describe this, Pat replied: "It's who I am. I am a spiritually integrated therapist and the care I offer is spiritually integrated. Counseling is a relationship and I bring my personal integration to that process." When asked about how she managed behavioral sciences and theology, she replied that she expected her counseling theories to be congruent with her personal sense of spiritual meaning, and that her spiritual meaning was sometimes altered by information from counseling theories and behavioral sciences. As an example she recalled her training program. Her supervisors challenged her theology in the light of client experience and information from psychotherapy models. They also challenged her to "think in theological categories" about diagnoses, therapeutic methods, and her relationship with clients. "There was always some kind of conversation about psychology and theology, or spirituality and therapy. The two were supposed to work together within the person of the counselor to provide a broader understanding of the client, counseling, and the therapeutic relationship."

Jeff O. works in an AAPC-accredited counseling center. He is licensed as a marriage and family therapist but identifies himself almost exclusively as a pastoral counselor. He holds a DMin degree in pastoral counseling. He was central in forming a "theological diagnosis and reflection group" that meets twice monthly in his agency. This group presents and reviews client cases. The stated agenda is to "explore the theological dynamics" related to client problems, diagnosis, and psychotherapeutic treatment. The group's goal is (1) to enrich the counselor's vision of the client or family by exploring theological themes associated with presenting problems and patterns of relating, (2) to use a form of "theological diagnosis" with clients to expand DSM-IV-TR[8] and family assessment of clients, and (3) to broaden treatment models with theological information gained through structured reflection. They also hope to expand theological understanding through careful attention to psychotherapeutic knowledge. The group has agreed to hold each other accountable for balancing psychotherapeutic language with theological and spiritual language, a task Jeff finds difficult. He reports it is easier to reflect on client cases through the eyes of psychotherapy, which offers more concrete language and is more familiar to many pastoral counselors than theological language.

Both Pat and Jeff describe a position of dialogue for relating theology and science. Barbour believes this position is more constructive than either independence or conflict. Dialogue expects that a mutually informing conversation between science and religion is possible because, ultimately, the two ask similar questions and use similar philosophical methodologies. Barbour takes this one step further. He suggests that the Christian doctrine of creation requires relating science and religion in some mutually constructive way. Creation proposes (1) God created both form and matter, (2) the universe is orderly, (3) the details of this order are known by observation, and (4) the created order (including humanity) is good and worthy of exploration but is not itself divine. These propositions legitimize science as a way to explore and describe God's creation. They also make space for science to raise questions that science itself cannot answer. According to theologian David Tracy,[9] there is a fundamental, implicit theological dimension to all scientific exploration and discovery. Scientific outcomes pose ethical questions that extend beyond discrete observation and define horizons of experience that can have only theological answers. On the other side, theologies are limited because they are products of specific histories and often cannot see beyond them. New questions raised by science can press theology into new territory and new theological constructs. Furthermore, when examined closely, scientific and theological methods share similarities. Both rely on models and paradigms that transcend objective observation. Scientific observation is theory laden and dependent on "creative imagination in which *analogies and models* often play a role."[10] These help scientists imagine what is not readily observable—a function not unlike religious imagination, which also relies on metaphors and models to describe what cannot be observed. Barbour notes that religion is not as subjective as commonly thought, and science is not as objective and disconnected from subjectivity as is often assumed. It too is bound by history experienced in a natural world. Both science and religion live in communities of shared paradigms; both are belief systems in their own way.

Dialogue allows mutually informing, creative correlation between behavioral sciences and theology. Don Browning provides an excellent example in *Religious Thought and the Modern Psychologies*. He calls his approach a revised correlational method because, unlike the work of neo-orthodoxy and Tillich, his approach allows science to inform theology in a more direct way. Browning argues that all psychological systems become a form of religion when they move from discrete, empirical observation and begin to help people order their lives. At this point, psychologies are in theological territory and must be judged by theological criteria of adequacy. Similarly, when theology makes a claim about human embodiment or mental and emotional functioning, it crosses into the realm of psychology and must be judged by scientific criteria of adequacy. Browning's pastoral theological vision is one of mutually informing correlation where psychology is enhanced by theology, and theology is enhanced by psychology.

Pastoral counseling has always been in a dialogical position with behavioral sciences and psychotherapy. Pastoral counseling texts by Oates, Hiltner, and Clinebell, for example, show great facility in moving carefully, but almost seamlessly, between behavioral sciences, psychotherapy, and theology. For Oates, pastoral counselors were to be bilingual in pastoral ministry and psychotherapy and capable of moving from one to the other with agility.[11] At certain times emphasis leans toward a priority for behavioral sciences, in other times toward a theological priority. Pastoral counselors expect theology to inform their psychotherapeutic practice, and they expect psychotherapy to inform theology and religious practice.

Research data confirm this observation. When asked about theology and psychotherapy, most pastoral counselors described "bringing the two together" in mutually informing ways, particularly at the point of client treatment. Most often this was described as a function of identity: "who I am" is an "integrated person" who has internalized a blend of psychotherapy and theology. When the nuances of these statements were explored, these pastoral counselors relied on an intuitive sense of correlation gained in formative training rather than a conscious method of ongoing critical conversations between theology and social sciences. Most striking, the primary dynamic of correlation was not between competing information from psychotherapy and theology (or religion and behavioral sciences) but between the personal identity *of the therapist* and information from *both* theology and behavioral sciences. Decisions about the adequacy of both theory and theology were judged based on congruity with the pastoral counselor's internalized identity. Nancy Ramsay's work in pastoral diagnosis—an excellent example of the dialogue position—suggests this is no surprise. She states that the fundamental tasks of pastoral counseling rely on a highly dynamic, collaborative, and contextual way of knowing that is centered in the values and assumptions that make up pastoral identity. Consequently, pastoral counselors name reality through a particular worldview. This worldview is a "self-conscious assimilation to a dynamic unity of [the pastoral counselor's] embodied, affective, intellectual, spiritual, relational, priestly/professional, and cultural/historical self."[12] It becomes the primary interpretive lens through which theology, behavioral sciences, counseling tasks, and client experience are viewed. It is the internalized authority against which other information is correlated. A very small minority of pastoral counselors reported that they practiced second-order critical analysis[13] of the interaction between theology, religious practices, or spirituality and their favored psychotherapeutic theories.

Integration

David W. is staff therapist in a large metropolitan social service agency. He identifies himself as a pastoral counselor and Licensed Clinical Social

Worker. Religiously he is a "progressive Baptist." He reports that he is daily faced with a multicultural, interreligious context that defies the internal logic he gained in his pastoral counselor training program. He sometimes feels overwhelmed by complex client problems, new information from medical and psychiatric communities, and a plurality of attitudes about spirituality, religion, and theology. When asked how he relates behavioral sciences and theology, he responded: "I have to think very carefully about how these relate, especially when it comes to meeting such diverse clients. I can't assume that my own internalized values, the assumptions I learned in training, or even the theories I learned in training will have any relevance to the client I am about to see. I've had to let go of believing I intuitively know how to respond. This means that I have to carry on an integrative conversation with every case I see. I have to listen to the wisdom clients bring with them. I have to evaluate how these theories are culturally bound and have power in counseling relationships. I have to attend to how that works with any given case. The same is true of theology—theology is culture bound and privileges some people's reality over others. All told, I find myself in new territory a lot. This forces me to think carefully about how diagnosis, treatment methods, theological truth, and personal spirituality are created in social contexts and how they act in therapy. So, if I am working with a particular client, say, an African American single mom, I have to start with what she knows about herself, make no assumptions that I know anything about her or her experience. Then I have to listen to as many voices as possible so my client and I can arrive at a place of mutually defined 'reality' that allows us to work together. In this particular case, I would listen especially carefully to the voices of feminist, womanist, and African American theologians. These would help me understand her context, but they also vastly broaden my vision of what it means to be human and not let me get bogged down in any particular theory. Hopefully, that will keep me humble. I would also listen to social policies and community voices that impact her life daily and partly define her experience of herself. In the end, I guess we are constructing a new reality together that is theologically grounded and changes us both. I hope that gives us a language to empower her and maybe even change social contexts that impact her. Bottom line, I guess I think that's what theology is all about.

"I think I approach theory and theology in kind of the same way. They are both socially constructed and context-driven systems. I don't really think one has authority over the other. Together they construct a believable

'truth' that is workable in particular contexts. When the context changes, 'truth' has to change too. They inform each other, but neither is definitive without the other. I've been pretty influenced by process theology. I expect God to lure us toward novelty and harmony in theology and science."

David's response is one illustration of the integration position that looks for a direct relationship between theology and scientific theory that lets the content of theology be systematically integrated into the content of science. The dialogue position allows information to cross and enrich the knowledge of both science and theology, but it also maintains a firm boundary between the two. Integration softens this boundary to encourage convergence of scientific and theological knowledge. Since there is one creation, and theology and science are interpreting the same creation, there must be coherence between theological statements about creation and scientific observation. However, natural observation and the technologies produced by science raise moral and ethical questions that demand a similar coherence.

Barbour identifies two integrative theological methods. Natural theology is a way of creating theological statements based on natural observation. God's nature and existence can be inferred from the design of the natural order. Science describes this design. This has been a popular method since Thomas Aquinas's work in the thirteenth century. It has contemporary expressions in theologian Teilhard de Chardin and scientific concepts like the anthropic principle,[14] the directionality of evolution, and propositions that order in nature implies a Mind or a Designer behind natural history. Barbour suggests these have great appeal in a religiously plural world because theology can be based in scientific data upon which people agree, regardless of cultural and religious differences. However, natural theology is limited. Ideas of Impersonal Mind and Designer implied by natural observation do not explain the active, personal God central to religious communities. They also fail to produce images of God and community that sustain pastoral counseling.

According to Barbour, a theology of nature is more promising. It "starts from the life of a religious community and asks how its beliefs may need to be reformulated in the context of modern science."[15] It is anchored in historical revelation and religious experience but insists that theological statements, particularly those about God's nature and the human person, must be consistent with scientific evidence that nature is ecological, interdependent, and multileveled. These characteristics inform theological understanding of God's relationship to nature and human interactions with nature, including how human systems work. Barbour sees particular promise in process theism as a theological method that can produce a systematic synthesis—or a coherent metaphysical worldview—between science and theology. Process theism discerns creation as a long, incomplete process in which God interacts reciprocally with the world toward creation. This makes room for mutual scientific and theological explanations of natural phenomena. As an example, Barbour points to Birch and Cobb's[16] ecological theological model that integrates biology, process philosophy, and Christian thought. It envisions a just and sustainable society through interdependent communities of life.

Pastoral counselors have a rich history of taking an integrative approach to behavioral sciences and theology. Natural theology is implicit in early texts. Psychoanalysis and new psychological discoveries in the late nineteenth and early twentieth centuries influenced theologies of God and human nature upon which pastoral practices were formed. There are many recent examples of how pastoral theologians have moved toward a systematic synthesis of behavioral sciences and theology to describe human behavioral and psychological life and guide pastoral counseling. Examples can be found in the work of Carroll Wise, Howard Clinebell, Archie Smith Jr., Edward Wimberly, Larry Graham, Bonnie Miller-McLemore, James Ashbrook, Nancy Ramsay, Pamela Cooper-White, and Christie Cozad Neuger, to name just a few. Some, like Barbour, appropriate process theism; all begin, as Barbour suggests, "from the life of a religious community" and ask "how its beliefs may need to be reformulated in the context of modern science." In recent years, pastoral counselors' exploration of human life has expanded from behavioral sciences into other natural sciences such as ecology[17] and neuroscience.[18] Integration is also reflected in the field's move toward communal-contextual paradigms that consider ecological, interdependent, and multileveled theological visions of human life.

Few research respondents in daily, full-time pastoral counseling practice talked about integration as a systematic synthesis of behavioral sciences and theology. Integration for most meant "personally integrated." When present, systematic synthesis was most often an artifact of a particular supervisor and not a deliberate reflective position of the counselor. Exceptions were pastoral counselors who had written a PhD or DMin thesis with this focus, and several who worked in medical or academic contexts that demanded conscientious thought about the relationship between theology and behavioral sciences.

Conflict

Pastoral counselors rarely take this position. It assumes an irresolvable conflict between science and religion, sometimes described as open warfare.[19] Here science and religion make competing, literal statements about the same natural domain. This forces an uncompromising choice, often between scientific materialism and biblical literalism. Scientific materialism takes a rigid stand based on the dual assumption that only the scientific method can produce reliable knowledge and that the reality of the universe is restricted to matter. Religious knowledge, spiritual experience, and belief are fundamentally unreliable because these cannot be verified with experimentally testable data. E. O. Wilson,[20] for instance, uses human evolution and neuroscience to show that human morality, spirituality, and religion are genetic artifacts of human survival that will disappear when they are no longer needed. Materialist philosophers[21] assert that all mental events, including human consciousness and religious belief, must be explained by the same physical laws that govern any other natural phenomenon. Barbour states that, despite its power in Western culture, scientific materialism is flawed because it fails "to distinguish between *scientific* and *philosophical* questions"[22] and has become an alternative belief system claiming universal truth. This truth relies entirely on impersonal concepts and is a form of reductionism that leaves out the most distinctive features of personal life. It is a belief system in clear conflict with theistic religion.

Biblical literalism claims that Scripture is inerrant throughout and is the final judge of all knowledge, including scientific knowledge. This claim was the force behind the Scopes trial in 1925, in which biblical literalists argued that evolution should not be taught in schools because it was contrary to Scripture.[23] More recently, biblical literalists have called for a creation science that explains natural phenomena in ways consistent with literal interpretation of the biblical texts. Where scientific materialism explains all phenomena as natural processes, biblical literalism rejects any scientific information that cannot be verified by a biblical text.

These two positions are reflected in contemporary counseling practices. Scientific materialism is evident in the work of mental health professionals who explain all mental and emotional life exclusively as a function of neurobiology, genetics, and social environmental effects. Diagnosis and treatment assume the priority of observable, testable factors; counseling procedures are designed to manipulate behavior, belief, and biochemistry toward reduction of symptoms. For these practitioners, there is little space for religion, spirituality, or faith apart from its adaptive function in evolution, its ability to help clients cope with uncooperative biochemistry, or its influence on behavior that will impact the material foundations of social or biochemical problems.

Biblical literalism is expressed in the biblical counseling movement and in religious traditions that discourage any form of counseling in favor of strict religious practices. Biblical counselors reject all behavioral sciences and psychotherapy and claim these are humanistic, devoid of God, and part of an anti-Christian culture of materialism. The Bible, read literally, is totally sufficient and the only source of authority in all matters of human life and behavior. It holds the answer to any problem that individuals, couples, families, or communities will encounter. A biblical counselor's task is to lead counselees to appropriate scripture and help them implement it in their lives. While some make room for biochemical problems, they also assert that behavioral and psychiatric diagnoses (such as bipolar disorder, ADD, depression, and personality disorders) can be a mask to disguise problems of the heart or ineffective Christian living. As a result, medical diagnoses must be unpacked to reveal these more foundational problems.[24] This view places all mental, emotional, and psychological problems squarely in the religious realm and accessible to biblical intervention. However, " 'cure' is not the aim of biblical counsel, instead it is conformity to the image of Jesus Christ (sanctification). Teach counselees the significance of eternal focus versus temporal focus."[25] This assumes a sharp dualism between mind (or soul) and body that is rejected by most Christian counselors and pastoral counselors.

Biblical counseling is a thriving movement in fundamentalist Christianity. It has replaced both pastoral counseling and Christian counseling in numerous conservative evangelical universities and seminaries. Russell Moore at Southern Baptist Theological Seminary, home of pastoral counseling pioneer Wayne Oates, summarizes this agenda. He contends that the CPE/pastoral care and counseling model was "founded on a theological worldview and ministry paradigm inconsistent with the theological worldview and conversionist outlook of the new era [of Southern Baptist conservative majority and Southern Seminary leadership]."[26] Psychotherapeutic language is used to "evade the biblical witness on issues of sin, righteousness, and judgment—the very issues that are at the heart of the gospel itself." Biblical counselors should be able to bring the mind of Christ to human problems in a way consistent with a biblical worldview. These should not be "outsourced" to clinical professionals informed by psychology, neurobiology, or other approaches that might neutralize or cover individual guilt. Moore rejects Christian counseling because it is tied to counseling methods and behavioral science information. It does not take seriously "the effects of the Adamic fall on the human race and its intellectual projects."[27] Because mental health professionalism shapes assumptions that work against faith, biblical counselors are not trained toward counseling licenses or professional identity. Instead, the New Testament teaches that the local congregation and its leadership are the "nexus of Kingdom activity" and the "vehicle for transforming individuals." This militates against any kind of parachurch or professional counseling. According to Moore, biblical counseling

> moves beyond the clinical professionalism of what has historically been dubbed "pastoral care" in the therapeutic guild, but it also means recovering true "pastoral care" as defined by the Scriptures.... These changes better equip pastors and church leaders to counsel the couple considering divorce ... to talk with the anorexic teenager ... [and] aid parents at the point of desper-

ation over a "strong-willed child." Above all...[it] equips our pastors and church leaders to trust the Word of truth.[28]

Barbour underscores that biblical literalism is a threat to both religious and scientific freedom. It may provide some security for believers in a time of rapid change, but its absolutist position may also breed intolerance and impose rigid religious views on others in a plural society.[29] Pastoral counselors rarely, if ever, approach their work as biblical literalists or as champions of the irrevocable conflict between science and religion. Research results revealed a number of religiously conservative and evangelical pastoral counselors. None described themselves as a biblical counselor, though most claimed they used the Bible as an important source of authority for their counseling without rejecting behavioral sciences.

Psychotherapy and Spirituality

In the study (WPC), comments such as "I practice spiritually integrated psychotherapy" had a variety of meanings. In most cases, pastoral counselors were referring to themselves as spiritually integrated personally. Their counseling embodied spirituality, even if they or clients never spoke of religious, spiritual, or faith issues. A number of these pastoral counselors used "theologically integrated" and "spiritually integrated" interchangeably. Several stated that they substituted "spiritually integrated" for "theologically integrated." They believed this appealed to a diverse public that does not understand "theologically integrated" or "pastoral counseling" but could identify with "spiritually based therapy."

A second common meaning for spiritually integrated referred to a specific form of therapy that consciously connected spirituality and psychology: "I work at the intersection of clients' spirituality and their psychological problems," or "I see myself as a therapist and spiritual caregiver." These counselors sometimes described themselves as "spiritual clinicians." Their expertise was "paying attention to the spiritual dimension" and balancing this with "good psychotherapy." While their personal spiritual identity was important, their larger concern was clinical competency in addressing spiritual issues in therapy. For most of these counselors, spirituality was interpreted as a natural dimension of every person.

Pastoral counseling was "spiritually integrated" when it addressed "big picture" questions or universal human issues of mystery, purpose, and meaning. Their goal in therapy was to improve emotional and psychological health and strengthen spirituality by working where these two human dimensions met.

This is consistent with an explosion in interdisciplinary literature instructing counselors how to identify and address client spirituality. Psychologist William Miller describes this as a "scientist-practitioner" approach that "values the scientific method as a way of knowing and the spiritual side of human nature that eludes reductionism."[30] He points out that clients deserve the best that science has to offer, but clients also bring with them a spiritual world of "meaning, seeking, believing, and wondering." This world is central to the way in which many clients understand their lives. Miller goes on to define spirituality as an individual attribute, similar to other psychological attributes. It is not the same as religion, which is an organized social entity, but religiosity may be an expression of spirituality for many clients. Spirituality operates independently of religion as a "multidimensional space" across three separate psychological domains: practice, belief, and experience. Each of these can be assessed and measured using a number of spiritual assessment instruments now available. Miller observes that spiritual issues can be incorporated into psychotherapy approaches without dramatically reshaping them. This makes psychotherapy more accessible to clients for whom spirituality is important. Psychiatrist Len Sperry[31] has proposed a model of spiritually attuned psychotherapy that is equally concerned about reduction of symptoms and spiritual growth. Sperry interprets pastoral counseling as a discipline more concerned with psychotherapy and psychological health for religious people than integrating spirituality and counseling. He offers his model as an alternative that centralizes spirituality.

Miller's and Sperry's approaches represent a broad movement in the clinical disciplines to attend to spirituality as an important category of experience and as a protective factor for human well-being. Several disciplines have identified a set of competencies that counselors need to engage clients' spiritual concerns.[32] Empirical and clinical study of spirituality and psychotherapy suggests that integration of spirituality with psychotherapy is pan-theoretical—

that is, spirituality can be integrated into most psychotherapy theories and practice. This observation does not lend support to some pastoral counselors' claim that depth psychology or psychodynamic theory is necessary for spiritual integration. Spirituality studies are important because they are defining the complex interface between faith and mental health, spirituality and coping, and religious practices and healing.

Pastoral counselors have not been central to this clinical and scientific study of spirituality, but it has had a direct impact on the field. This universal, psychological understanding of spirituality forms the structure of interdisciplinary conversations in which pastoral counselors participate, grants credibility to pastoral counselors' claim that they treat the spiritual dimension of people's lives, and provides a context for claiming that pastoral counselors (among other therapists) offer holistic care. It is interesting, however, that pastoral counselors do not report using the multiple empirical tools this research has developed for spiritual assessment (for example, Spiritual Well-Being Scale, God Imagery Inventory,[33] etc.). Instead, they rely primarily on their intuitive sense of the client's spirituality or the client's spiritual self-report. Pastoral counselors may benefit from better acquaintance with these tools. Although this research has had a number of positive effects for pastoral counselors, pastoral theologian Herbert Anderson[34] voices caution about embracing this individualistic understanding of spirituality. Pastoral counselors may be joining a larger cultural revolution to recognize mystery, universal longing for meaning, and connections between spirituality and health, but in the process they may also abandon the substance of spirituality tied to an identifiable community of faith and practice. This divorces pastoral counseling from its historic roots and is a shaky foundation for the future of the field. He urges careful, critical theological evaluation of how pastoral counselors identify themselves in this movement.

A small minority of pastoral counselors talked about spirituality in psychotherapy as directly related to the spirit of God in session and engaging the beliefs and practices of the client's specific religious community. In these cases, pastoral counselors saw themselves as spiritual guides and referred to therapy sessions as "holy ground." Spirituality was not a "dimension" of human life but a communal connection, an expression of God's activity, and the guiding structure for the whole of the person's religious and psychological life. Spiritual intervention was their primary concern. Psychotherapy was a way to assist spiritual guidance. These counselors almost always drew their clients from particular faith communities, or practiced in a way that highlighted their own religious connections and spiritual focus. Some were evangelical Protestants; others, Episcopal, Unitarian, or Catholic. Most reported that they talked about specific religious issues, church relationships, doctrines, scripture references, and spiritual practices in session. Several reported that they prayed regularly for their clients as a matter of their own spiritual practice. Some prayed with clients in session.

Several African American pastoral counselors gave striking examples of this approach to spirituality and psychotherapy. These therapists believed that such an explicit approach to spirituality in life and therapy was necessary for counseling African American clients. One therapist summarized:

"When I sit down with African American clients, we have a particular relationship. We are African American. We are brothers and sisters. We have a common faith. My clients believe, whatever they call God. They utilize that faith to live. They may be Methodist, they may be Christian, or not, but we share the same thing. It doesn't matter what you call God, because we have the same struggle. We connect in suffering. There is a common historical perspective where we all come from suffering, be it racism, classism or whatever. And so there is an automatic commonality, for instance, talking about being in an abusive relationship and feeling no options. We have a connection in being powerless. Somehow, soul to soul, we connect. Something occurs between the therapist and the client, and then there is the Spirit that interprets on both sides. If that is really working, that's where healing occurs. I believe that everything originates in spirit and I think the various crises we are in are because of the various social 'isms' that cloud us. But we are all seeking to get back to spirit, get back to a connection. Ed Wimberly talks about the relational refugee, how we are just kind of floating around and we are seeking to get connected to something. So when clients come into my office I think pastoral counseling provides a curative for the wandering soul. As I began to develop and find my way into a more Afri-centered approach to pastoral counseling, I

really connected myself with African spirituality. I exist because you exist and we constantly seek that connection. After a while therapy technique and the seeing of clients over and over are not satisfying. What is satisfying is the excitement that every time you go into the room the Spirit might show up.... The miracle is you just don't know when it's going to show up and that's what I mean by the Spirit. You never know when that manifestation that we can actually touch, feel, and see will show up."

Another African American pastoral counselor concluded:

"I don't believe, as a pastoral counselor, I can treat African American clients apart from the shared spirituality of the African American community and the Black church experience.... You cannot understand the life, suffering, and healing of African American clients apart from these. I believe it's rooted in African spirituality that takes life in the spirit world, the influence of ancestors, and our commonality seriously. So that's where you have to start. You have to be explicit about this spiritual ground in counseling. Psychotherapy has to start there."

These responses are consistent with the work of African American theologians and African American pastoral theologians.[35]

A very small minority of pastoral counselors defined themselves also as spiritual directors or spiritual life-coaches. These counselors prioritized spiritual growth with a focus on clients' relationship with God and religious community and upon life crises that affected spiritual life. They reported using structured spiritual practices as interventions. One counselor interviewed was certified both as a pastoral counselor and as a spiritual director. These counselors rejected neutrality in therapy and engaged clients in a way that valued the client's spiritual values and the therapist's personal spiritual life and commitments. Interaction between counselor and client was considered a collaborative venture toward the client's health and well-being. One pastoral counselor saw great promise for this model of pastoral counseling, particularly as it intersected with postmodern theories that value indigenous spiritual information, that confront the limitations of psychotherapeutic theory, and that call for true collaboration between clients and therapists.

Conclusion

What do pastoral counselors do? Pastoral counselors organize their thoughts and behavior around personal identity, and they integrate theology and behavioral sciences, spirituality and psychotherapy. However, integration is a nontechnical and sometimes ambiguous idea for most pastoral counselors. It rarely embodies Barbour's definition: a method of systematically synthesizing information from religious and spiritual sources with information from behavioral sciences and psychotherapy. Instead, it refers to a pastoral counselor's personal sense of congruence between different kinds of knowledge. As one pastoral counselor stated, "It is the *pastoral counselor* who has to be integrated. I guess it's important at some level to know what psychotherapy says and what theology says, but in the end it is *me* and how I've internalized my training that forms a relationship with the client." Most pastoral counselors gained a sense of congruence by internalizing particular assumptions and practices while in training. Pastoral counselors spoke of "spiritually integrated therapy" in equally nontechnical and personal ways. "Spiritually integrated" most often referred to a sense of internalized congruence between the counselor's spirituality and what takes place in counseling sessions. Examined closely, counselors' descriptions of congruence usually reflected one of Barbour's models (independence, dialogue, or integration). However, this was complicated by elusive and widely divergent definitions of *spiritual, spirituality,* and *spiritually integrated.*

There is great strength in the pastoral counselor's sense that boundaries between behavioral sciences and theology, spirituality and psychotherapy, are organized by personal pastoral identity. However, integration of psychotherapy and spirituality, for instance, defined primarily as internal congruity with personal identity also holds a substantial liability, particularly if critical analysis takes a backseat to intuitive judgment. It was striking that many research respondents could describe *why* integration of behavioral sciences and theology, psychotherapy and spirituality, was important. They could not, however, describe *how* they did this apart from intuitive judgment. In the plural world in which pastoral counselors now live, it is a matter of professional integrity to be able to articulate theologically and methodologically how we bring religious information, theology, spirituality and behavioral sciences together. This is critically important as pastoral counselors move beyond the shared assumptive world of a specific religious community, enter pluralistic public institutions, and join in public discourse about social policy.

Notes

1. For a more complete discussion of pastoral theology definition, see: Nancy Ramsay, "A Time of Ferment and Redefinition," in *Pastoral Care and Counseling: Redefining the Paradigms,* ed. Nancy Ramsay (Nashville: Abingdon Press, 2004).

2. Ian Barbour, *Religion and Science* (New York: HarperSanFrancisco, 1990); Ian Barbour, *When Science Meets Religion* (New York: HarperSanFrancisco, 2000).

3. Barbour, *Religion and Science,* 84.

4. Gilkey testified as an expert witness for the American Civil Liberties Union challenging a law passed by the Arkansas legislature mandating that creation science be taught on equal footing with evolution in high schools. He argued that the creation science of biblical literalism was not science, but religion cloaked as science.

5. Langdon Gilkey, *Creationism on Trial* (Minneapolis: Winston Press, 1985).

6. Don S. Browning, *Religious Thought and the Modern Psychologies* (Minneapolis: Fortress Press, 1987/2004).

7. For example, see Eric L. Johnson, *Foundations for Soul Care: A Christian Psychology Proposal* (Downers Grove, Ill.: IVP Press, 2007).

8. DSM-IV-TR refers to American Psychiatric Association, *Diagnostic and Statistical Manual of Mental Disorders-IV-TR,* 4th, text revision ed. (Washington, D.C.: American Psychiatric Association, 2000). This is the standard document for diagnosing mental illness in the United States.

9. David Tracy, *Blessed Rage for Order* (New York: Seabury, 1975).

10. Barbour, *When Science Meets Religion,* 90, italics in original.

11. Mark Wingfield, "Pastoral Counseling's Pioneer Recalls His Experiences," *Western Recorder,* November 3, 1998.

12. Nancy Ramsay, *Pastoral Diagnosis: A Resource for Ministries of Care and Counseling* (Minneapolis: Fortress Press, 1998), 103.

13. First-order analysis is a pastoral counselor's ability to describe the fact that he or she brings these elements together. Second-order critical analysis is the pastoral counselor's ability to analyze *how* she or he has gone about bringing together these various sources.

14. The anthropic principle is a cosmological argument based on astrophysical evidence that life in the universe would have been impossible if conditions in the early universe had varied even slightly. Stephen Hawking in *A Brief History of Time* ([New York: Bantam Books, 1988], 291) concluded: "If the rate of expansion

one second after the big bang had been smaller by even one part in a hundred thousand million million, the universe would have recollapsed before it ever reached its present size." This observation allows a theological argument for Mind that "fine tuned" the universe toward life and human existence.

15. Barbour, *When Science Meets Religion*, 37.

16. Charles Birch and John B. Cobb Jr., *The Liberation of Life* (Cambridge: Cambridge University Press, 1981).

17. Howard Clinebell, *Ecotherapy: Healing Ourselves, Healing the Earth* (Minneapolis: Fortress Press, 1996).

18. James B. Ashbrook and Carol R. Albright, *The Humanizing Brain: Where Religion and Neuroscience Meet* (Cleveland: Pilgrim Press, 1997); James B. Ashbrook, *Minding the Soul: Pastoral Counseling as Remembering* (Minneapolis: Fortress Press, 1996); David A. Hogue, *Remembering the Future, Imagining the Past: Story, Ritual, and the Human Brain* (Cleveland: Pilgrim Press, 2003).

19. Barbour (*When Science Meets Religion*, 10) cites John W. Draper, *History of the Conflict between Religion and Science* (New York: Appleton, 1874), and Andrew D. White, *A History of the Warfare between Science and Religion* (New York: Appleton, 1896), to illustrate how conflict between science and religion became a popular idea in American culture.

20. Edward O. Wilson, *On Human Nature* (Cambridge: Harvard University Press, 1978).

21. Daniel Dennett, *Consciousness Explained* (New York: Little Brown, 1991).

22. Barbour, *Religion and Science*, 81, italics in original.

23. *Scopes v. State of Tennessee*, 152 Tenn. 424, 278 S.W. 57 (Tenn. 1925) was a case testing a Tennessee law (the Butler Act) that forbade teaching any theory in a public institution that denied divine creation of "man" as taught by the Bible. The trial featured three-time presidential candidate Williams Jennings Bryan, who prosecuted high school teacher John Scopes, and Clarence Darrow, who defended Scopes. Though the court was unsure whether he had actually taught evolution in his science classes, Scopes was convicted and fined. In a later appeal, the Tennessee Supreme Court upheld the Butler Act as constitutional but reversed Scopes's conviction on procedural grounds. The Butler Act was repealed in 1967.

24. Some biblical counselors allow room for medical psychiatric problems that require medical treatment. However, counselors must distinguish which problems in living may be nonmoral, biological problems and which are related to moral problems and religious lifestyle. A similar dichotomy is implicit. Medical science is good and appropriate to human care, but behavioral or psychological sciences are not.

25. Association of Biblical Counselors, http://www.christiancounseling.com/attachments/wysiwyg/4/Diagnosticdisclaimerfinal2.pdf (accessed July 3, 2008).

26. Russell Moore, "Counseling and the Authority of Christ: A New Vision for Biblical Counseling at Southern Baptist Theological Seminary" (Louisville: Southern Baptist Theological Seminary, 2005).

27. Ibid., 7.

28. Ibid., 11.

29. Barbour, *Religion and Science*.

30. William Miller, *Integrating Spirituality into Treatment: Resources for Practitioners* (Washington, D.C.: American Psychological Association, 2000), xiii.

31. Len Sperry, *Spirituality in Clinical Practice* (Philadelphia: Brunner-Routledge, 2001).

32. CACREP, "Council on Accreditation of Counseling and Related Educational Programs" (Alexandria, Va.: Council on Accreditation of Counseling and Related Educational Programs, 2001); G. Miller, "The Development of Spiritual Focus in Counseling and Counselor Education," *Journal of Counseling and Development* 77 (1999); J. S. Young et al., "Spiritual and Religious Competencies: A National Survey of CACREP Accredited Programs," *Counseling and Values* 47, no. 1 (2002).

33. C. Ellison, *Spiritual Well-Being Scale* (Nyack, N.Y.: Life Advance, 1994); R. T. Lawrence, "Measuring the Image of God: The God Image Inventory and the God Image Scales," *Journal of Psychology and Theology* 25, no. 2 (1997).

34. Herbert Anderson, "Spiritual Care: The Power of an Adjective," *Journal of Pastoral Care* 55, no. 3 (2001).

35. See the work of Edward Wimberly, Archie Smith Jr., Homer Ashby, Thomas Pugh, and womanist theologian Elaine Crawford, among many others.

CHAPTER 5

Forming Transforming Relationships

Pastoral counselors act as agents of transformation by forming therapeutic relationships that help people change or cope with things that cannot change. Chapter 4 explored how pastoral counselors relate behavioral sciences and theology. In this chapter we turn to examine how pastoral counselors apply this integration and work with clients toward transformation. This chapter is based on four questions.

1. What do pastoral counselors *do* in counseling?
2. How is this guided by theory?
3. Since pastoral counseling borrows its psychotherapy methods from other disciplines, how does counseling retain its pastoral nature?
4. Recent psychotherapy research challenges some of pastoral counseling's long-held assumptions about psychotherapy and "how it works." How does this research inform pastoral counseling practice or change its practice?

Throughout the chapter, I will use case studies to illustrate how ideas translate into practice.

Denise M. has been a pastoral counselor for fifteen years. She completed her training while serving as a parish pastor in a small congregation. Ten years ago, she entered private practice and continued to serve as a part-time parish minister. She values her experience as a parish pastor and the more "in-depth" work she now does with clients who are not her parishioners. Denise defines pastoral counseling as a "transformative relationship" made possible by her identity but that is acted out (she also uses the

word "embodied") through her use of psychotherapeutic theory. Her theory guides her use of specific skills such as creating a therapeutic alliance, assessing clients, treatment planning, "working through the issues," and helping clients "claim and maintain transformation." She considers herself a "psychodynamically oriented" therapist and talks about how she has integrated psychodynamic theory and therapy practices into her pastoral identity. These provide the primary lens through which she views problems and transformation.

Dan R. was certified as a pastoral counselor five years ago. He completed his training in a university that offered a degree in pastoral counseling. He is a licensed marriage and family therapist and works in a Samaritan Center. Like Denise, Dan identifies pastoral counseling as a "special kind of relationship" in which counselor and client join in a "rich, spiritual connection" that helps clients change problematic relationships, feelings, and behaviors. Though trained in "a more Rogerian theory," Dan did not experience this as congruent with his own values or experiences. After graduation he enrolled in a solution-focused training program and found this model of therapy more consistent with his beliefs, his own experience of change, and his assumptions about God's creative action in the world. He believed that his pastoral identity was enriched by having to "think through" how solution-focused therapy interacted with his theological commitments, his vision of the human person, and his disagreements with other pastoral counselors about his choice of theory. When discussing his work, Dan spoke about his "pastoral presence" with clients in much the same way as Denise. He believes that change is the result of the client-therapist relationship, that his work embodies his identity, and that together these empower clients to change. Consistent with his theory, he does not believe that change relies on "in-depth personality work" or assumptions of personal pathology. As in Denise's case, his theory and skills guide how he establishes a therapeutic alliance, assesses problems, plans treatment, and evaluates change.

Pastoral counselors see their work as an extension of personal identity formed in training and reflective experience. Identity expresses purpose: pastoral counselors provide counseling, pastoral psychotherapy, or spiritually integrated psychotherapy to individuals, couples, families, or institutions in need of behavioral, cognitive, emotional, social, or spiritual transformation. This purpose requires counseling theory and skill. Though most pastoral counselors interviewed claimed pastoral counseling was a "way of being in relationship" rather than a set of skills, the same people also insisted that pastoral counselors must be highly skilled therapists. Denise and Dan, in the vignettes above, illustrate how pastoral counselors assimilate theory into their identity and use it to construct a conceptual frame.

Which theory(ies) should be integrated into pastoral counselor identity has not always been a terribly significant question for pastoral counselors. For much of its institutional history, pastoral counseling simply assumed psychodynamic or Rogerian methods. This was reflected in AAPC individual and training center certification standards, certification committee practices, and themes of AAPC's conferences. In his review of fifty years of literature, pastoral theologian Howard Stone noted that pastoral counselors often overlooked new developments in psychotherapy in favor of "seemingly endless variations of early twentieth-century therapeutic [psychodynamic and Rogerian] approaches."[1] This finding is not surprising. The field emerged when psychoanalytic therapy was one of two or three available methods, Carl Rogers was an early recipient of AAPC's Distinguished Contribution Award, and training has been largely based on apprenticeship models that value intergenerational tradition over innovation. These factors have restricted the field by obscuring new methods useful to pastoral counseling and limiting the kinds of services available for clients. My own study of pastoral counselors' practices (WPC) showed that psychodynamic and Rogerian models continue to be favored. However, digging for a deeper maximum variation sample produced another group of counselors who identified their primary guiding theories as cognitive, behavioral, solution-focused, collaborative, Bowenian, structural family therapy, strategic therapy, narrative therapy, and multicultural therapy. Many counselors who identified themselves as psychodynamic therapists also claimed a "secondary modality" that informed their work with couples, families, or special populations. Counselors trained outside programs with historic ties to psychoanalytic practice and non-AAPC members were more likely to claim alternative theories and to talk about their guiding theories in more flexible ways.

Therapy Models and Change

A substantial body of research has shown that people with mental health problems or problems in living improve more quickly when they receive psychotherapy. There has also been substantial disagreement between influential leaders and therapists about what model of therapy is best. Since the time of Freud, therapy theories and models have proliferated. In 1986 one observer[2] estimated that more than four hundred different approaches were available to psychotherapists, and that this number was continuing to expand. Despite this rapid expansion and anecdotal claims that new therapies improve outcome, extensive research[3] has failed to demonstrate any difference in effectiveness between various psychotherapeutic models. Furthermore, claims that long-term therapy facilitates deeper or more lasting change over short-term therapy have not been supported, though there is evidence that a minority of clients need and will benefit from longer-term therapy.[4]

These and other studies suggest that the therapy model a pastoral counselor chooses is less important than several other factors common to all successful counseling. In his landmark 1961 book *Persuasion and Healing,*[5] psychiatrist Jerome Frank compared psychotherapy with religious healing, preindustrial magical healing, and the placebo effect in medicine. He observed that culture produces the distress that drives people to healers. It defines what behavior, feelings, and thoughts are normal and how variance is to be understood. When a culture explains difference or ordinary unhappiness as an illness, then problems need "treatment" rather than some other kind of response.[6] People who seek psychotherapy in Western culture are those who "experience various degrees of helplessness, hopelessness, confusion, and subjective incompetence"[7] because they are unable to manage a problem in a "normal" way. When this is persistent, an individual's meaning system is impaired and her or his assumptive world fails to match circumstances. This leads to demoralization, the sense that one is powerless to change one's self or life circumstances. Demoralized people consult psychotherapists because they are socially sanctioned healers who are expected to combat demoralization and help clients transform their lives.

In Frank's analysis, psychotherapy is a form of rhetorical persuasion that works to transform or find new plots for client stories.
People feel better when therapy helps them modify their assumptive world and transform "pathogenic meanings to ones that rekindle hope, enhance mastery, heighten self-esteem, and reintegrate
patients with their groups."[8] Transformation requires four elements: (1) an emotionally charged confiding relationship with a
helping person, (2) a healing setting, (3) a rational, conceptual
scheme or myth that provides a plausible explanation for the
client's symptoms and prescribes a ritual for resolving them, and
(4) a ritual or procedure that requires the active participation of
both client and therapist and is believed by both to be effective for
restoring health. These are the active ingredients in all psychotherapy, revivalism, preindustrial religious-magical healing, and the
placebo effect in general medicine.

More recent studies confirm that change in counseling is related
to factors other than psychotherapy model or technique.
Lambert's[9] 1992 analysis of outcome studies refines Frank's observations. Lambert identifies four factors that account for change in
psychotherapy:

- Client-therapist relationship variables (an emotionally charged
  relationship and healing setting) account for about 30 percent
  of positive outcomes in therapy;
- Client variables or extratherapeutic factors (client motivation
  and active participation in ritual, client belief system, and environmental support) account for about 40 percent of change;
- Fifteen percent of client change is determined by hope, or the
  client's expectation that things can change; and
- Fifteen percent of change in therapy is related to application of
  a therapeutic model (explanatory myth and healing rituals).
  Hubble, Duncan, and Miller[10] suggest that all therapy models
  and techniques share a common quality—they all prepare
  clients to take action on their own behalf.

Lambert's conclusions and others' appropriation of them (particularly Hubble, Duncan, and Miller) provide a pan-theoretical
framework for understanding what counselors do to facilitate
transformation in clients' lives. This may be particularly important

for pastoral counselors who tend toward intense commitment to a favored theory that is assimilated into personal identity and given theological power. These studies encourage humility about theories and the role that pastoral counselors play in clients' lives. Therapeutic models account for only a small percentage of client change, and successful therapy appears to be more about *client involvement* than counselor power.

Thirty Percent Factor: Pastoral Counseling and Client-Counselor Relationship

Frank's and Lambert's research largely supports what pastoral counselors have always claimed: "It's not about counseling technique; it's the relationship that heals." This has been a central icon of pastoral counselor training and formation. It has driven expectations that pastoral counselors must be personally and religiously integrated, successful in their own personal therapy, and able to demonstrate to certification committees that they could form and maintain a certain kind of relationship. Data (WPC) show that pastoral counselors work from an internalized religious-spiritual frame of reference that values relationship with the client above any other single factor in therapy. Pastoral counselors believe they form a unique relationship with clients. More than three-quarters of those interviewed spontaneously called this "pastoral presence" and described it as a characteristic of the counselor's personal identity. It is the motivating factor that drives and contains interactions between client and counselor.

Pastoral Presence

Though pastoral counselors had difficulty defining *pastoral presence,* they generally agreed about two characteristics. First, pastoral presence is a mystery connected to God's spirit. It is closely tied to biblical and theological images of God whose presence sustains creation, Jesus the Good Shepherd, and Christ's incarnation in the world. Second, it was often described as a kind of perfected empathy. Pastoral presence cannot be seen, touched, or heard but is experienced in an emotional joining that allows "true connection" with clients, "understanding deeply from the heart," or "believing for the clients when they cannot themselves believe." Often counseling sessions were referred to as "holy ground" on which the client and counselor become "co-pilgrims on spiritual journey." Depending on the therapist's religious heritage, this connection was seen as a form of spiritual discipline (Catholic), part of emptying one's heart (Orthodox), being present on a deeply human, transcendent level (Unitarian-Universalist, Jewish), or an incarnation of the body of Christ (Protestant). Presence is the mystery—the presence of God—that heals. Some counselors perceived it as the mediator of the Holy that transcends technique or theory. A few respondents believed that pastoral presence was a product of their ordination and relationship with a faith community. Most saw it as an independent personal characteristic of the counselor that freed "pastoral" from ordination and religious leadership. In both cases, pastoral presence was an expression of the counselor's self in therapy. It is not contingent upon client request or the client's spirituality or religious tradition. By entering into a relationship with a pastoral counselor, clients consent to engaging pastoral presence. A sizable minority of interviewed counselors justified "relating pastorally" to clients outside of sessions. "I'm the only pastor they have" was a common comment for those who made hospital visits, attended funerals, or performed weddings for clients.

Images of pastoral presence were also influenced by pastoral counselors' favored psychotherapeutic theories. Psychodynamic theory clearly shaped how most counselors spoke of presence. Many described it as a "special kind of empathy." Others described presence in terms of transference, countertransference, object representation, or projection, or used images of reparative experience. On the one hand, psychodynamic language is attractive because it values multilayered human emotional experience, emotional attachment with therapists, and personal insight. On the other hand, it is embedded in a specific assumptive world that is not universally shared. This holds several liabilities. First, tying pastoral presence too closely to a psychodynamic assumptive world (or any theory's assumptive world) can privilege those who share the meanings and values of that world and disenfranchise those who do not. For instance, clients who want practical behavioral change, but do not value personal insight, may be deprived of presence if they cannot shift their assumptive world to match the therapist's. Others may want help with marital communication and experience the pastoral counselor's attempts to "understand deeply from the heart" as intrusive. A definition of pastoral presence narrowed by this kind of theoretical specificity can subtly "select out" clients who do not share the counselor's assumptive world. Research in empathy, the closest psychological term to pastoral presence, may broaden the notion of presence in important ways.

Pastoral Presence and Empathy

Jane was a fifty-three-year-old woman who came for therapy in the middle of an unexpected divorce. She described her pastoral counselor as "very caring," "a good listener," and "able to feel [her] deep pain." She stated: "I don't know what I would have done. I was at the point I couldn't speak for myself. David just seemed to feel my feelings. Sometimes he didn't say anything. In the silence I didn't have to say anything either. I just knew he understood. He sat with me, feeling with me, until I could find my own voice. I give him credit for helping me avoid a deep, deep depression."

Gary was a forty-two-year-old single parent. In his first session with Lynn, he described how he had dropped out of therapy with another pastoral counselor. "I just felt like it was useless. I tried to tell him how lost I was as a single dad, and he would ask me, 'How does that feel?' or 'What do you make of that?' Then he would just sit there like I was supposed to say something. I felt ripped off paying two dollars a minute to sit there with someone who didn't say anything. I finally told him I came to him for help and that those were stupid questions. I didn't go back after the first visit." Gary described his experience a month later after four sessions with Lynn: "I feel like she really gets it. She seems to know how I feel and sometimes she'll say, 'You must have been embarrassed' or something like that. Mostly, though, I'll tell her what I do with the kids and she helps me think about it—why did this work rather than that? One time she asked me, 'What do you think would work better?' I almost yelled at her—If I knew that I would have done it! She caught on really quickly. I really like it when she tells me about trying to manage her own kids. That makes me feel almost normal. We'll talk about what worked for her and then we'll kind of evaluate whether that might work for me. Those mean more to me than anything else I got out of counseling. I'll never regret seeing her or paying for those sessions."

The word *empathy* was coined in the mid-1800s by Robert Vischer, a German philosopher, to refer to human feelings projected onto the natural world. In the 1890s the term was expanded by Theodor Lipps to refer to the psychological process of discovering that others have selves. Freud found great affinity with Lipps's thought and refined the term to describe how humans understand others by putting ourselves in their places. For Freud, this was essential to the therapeutic relationship. Self psychologist Heinz Kohut further refined empathy to mean the ability to think and feel one's self into the inner life of another person.[11] Empathy is associated with client improvement, but it is a complex phenomenon. Bachelor,[12] for instance, concluded that what therapists offer as empathy often is not experienced by clients as empathy when it does not match the client's style of engagement. She observed that about 30 percent of clients respond to affective-toned empathic responses and "felt known" when the therapist "felt with me" or "truly understood and felt what I was experiencing." Nearly half of clients (44 percent) responded positively to cognitive-type empathic responses. These clients appreciated the therapist's accurate cognitive *perception* of feelings and motivations rather than "feeling with." The remainder of clients (24 percent) responded positively to either a collaborative or a nurturing type of empathy. Collaborative empathy refers to reciprocal exchange or a therapy partnership. This may include therapists working with clients as equal partners or sharing personal opinions and experiences as part of the therapy process. Clients who rejected affective-toned and cognitive-type empathic approaches often preferred connecting through collaboration. A small minority of clients responded primarily to nurturing empathy that expressed a therapist's supportive, attentive, and caring presence. It appears, states Bachelor, "that, from the client's perspective, there is no single, invariably facilitative, therapist empathic response."[13] If therapists rely on one normative understanding of empathy—and similarly, pastoral presence—they cannot respond to the breadth of client styles of knowing, relating, and responding.

Managing differences and expectations in empathy is critical in counseling across cultures. This is an area where pastoral counselors are almost certain to experience discrepancies between their assumptive world, their expectations about empathy and pastoral presence, and the client's assumptive world and expectations. In these cases, "to know the heart of the stranger" requires humility, careful evaluation of one's internalized expectations about empathy and presence, and the ability to collaborate across boundaries of difference. Postmodern theories of therapy can help understand empathy and pastoral presence in these circumstances. Harlene Anderson and Diane Gehart,[14] for example, understand empathy in a way that rejects any assumption that counselors can intuitively understand the client's world because of their identity, training, or formation. Empathy is constructed by reverence for the client's unique experience and a conversation that cocreates mutual understanding. Latin American therapists Sylvia London and Florence Rosenberg[15] expand this idea by suggesting that ethnic, gender, national background, and social class differences are so rich that all counseling is cross-cultural. Counselor responses must rely on the expertise of the client's indigenous knowledge and not the therapist's expert analysis or observation. "Not knowing" becomes a form of empathy. This, however, poses a liability. Although "not knowing" rejects professionally privileged knowledge in favor of indigenous knowledge, an individualistic focus may miss or minimize larger cultural oppression of which a client is not immediately aware. For example, pastoral psychologist Lee Butler uses psychohistorical analysis and Africentric psychology to show how African American individual and communal identity is formed by both America's slave history and African origins (Theory of African American Identity Formation).[16] Without this larger critical perspective, "not knowing" that relies on individual indigenous knowledge can unintentionally reinforce internalized racism. This same concern—reliance on individual knowledge without critical cultural analysis—is echoed for women, persons with class differences, and differences in sexual orientation. Empathy and pastoral presence may best be expressed as a qualified "not knowing" that rejects the privileged position of the therapeutic "expert" but takes seriously mutual exploration of larger formative cultural, racial, ethnic, gender, and class concerns.

Rethinking Pastoral Presence as the Basic Relational Quality in Pastoral Counseling

Research (WPC) results suggest that pastoral counselors are highly biased toward an affective-tone nurturing image of empathy and pastoral presence, possibly at the expense of cognitive and collaborative forms of empathy. This may fit client styles less than half the time and may limit the kinds of clients who benefit from pastoral counselors' services. Expanding the notion of pastoral presence in two ways is helpful. First, it may be better to describe pastoral presence as *a meaning-constructing interaction* between counselor and client and not an individual quality that the pastoral counselor brings to therapy for the client. What clients bring to the encounter—history, preferred ways of knowing, assumptive worlds, and emotional frameworks—is at least as important as the counselor's identity and use of self. To establish pastoral presence, the pastoral counselor's approach *must match* the client's preferred style. This approach will help pastoral counselors see differences and reject any assumptions that they can understand "deeply from the heart" or enter a "true connection" across cultural or other personal boundaries based on internalized knowledge from their own identities. Second, pastoral counselors' identity formation should include experience that affirms, embraces, and practices diverse styles of empathy and presence. Re-visioning pastoral presence in these ways may release pastoral presence from overreliance on one psychotherapeutic theory or notion of empathy. It may also reaffirm interactions such as "come let us reason together," therapeutic collaboration toward justice, mutual analysis of power, and shared spiritual commitments as important forms of pastoral presence.

Pastoral Counseling: It's the Relationship

Studies indicate that the therapeutic relationship itself is more powerful than any specific cognitive, behavioral, or psychodynamic therapeutic procedure. However, it is equally true that *client perception* of the relationship is most important. Therapists "cannot assume that their evaluation of the quality of the therapy climate corresponds to their clients' perceptions."[17] The counseling relationship must be cocreated between counselor and client. Clients who actively collaborate with their therapists in this relationship fare better in therapy.[18] When there is a discrepancy between client and therapist perception of the relationship, therapy is less successful and clients are more likely to drop out. Furthermore, this transforming relational power appears to expand when the relationship includes pastoral presence. The added religious and spiritual meanings of this interaction have a positive impact on therapy, especially when they are consistent with the client's worldviews, expectations, and religious history.[19]

Fifty-five Percent Factor: Client Factors and Hope

Though the therapeutic relationship is clearly significant in helping a client combat demoralization, it is not adequate by itself. Lambert's analysis shows that an effective therapeutic relationship accounts for about 30 percent of change, but what *clients* bring to counseling accounts for about 40 percent of client improvement, and hope an additional 15 percent.

The Client's Part of Counseling

Pastoral counseling literature tends to be professional centered. That is, it champions the person of the counselor, counselor skills, and *therapist*-generated events that benefit clients. However, a growing body of research suggests that humans live with a "powerful endogenous therapeutic system that is part of the psychophysiology of all individuals"[20] and that change is related more to client motivation and behavior than to what therapists do. It appears that all change is self-change. People regularly and independently overcome their problems and make changes in their lives; therapy is a form of professionally coached self-change.[21] The primary effect of counseling may be that it awakens clients' personal agency, focuses their effort for self-healing, and provides support for taking action on their own behalf.[22] Clients who are invested in counseling, expect that it will help, and have a clear sense of their goal are likely to experience transformation. These clients change regardless of their therapist's theoretical orientation, preferred interventions, and therapeutic errors. In fact, one series of studies[23] showed that *clients* direct their own successful therapy by covertly steering sessions, diverting therapists toward conversations they need to have, and ignoring therapists' technical errors. Clients use what is useful and reject what is not. Those who appear passive or resistant may, in fact, be very active but pursuing a different agenda for therapy than is their therapist.

When clients describe successful therapy, they refer to therapists who helped them share the load of their distress, gain self-understanding in the problem, and practice new thoughts and behaviors they could implement outside of sessions.[24] Therapists, it appears, provide a work space that supports a client's natural generativity with empathy, a coconstructive dialogue, direct experiential learning in therapy interactions, and coaching toward new skills.

Like most other therapists, pastoral counselors tend to overlook client variables and focus on the person, skills, and actions of the counselor as the primary change agent in therapy. This was particularly evident when pastoral counselors spoke about the pastoral relationship. Client contributions were rarely considered except in the case of two or three counselors who stated that the client "ordains" the counselor as a spiritual leader in the counseling process. For the most part, clients appear in both pastoral counseling literature and personal interviews as receivers of care.

Clients may be best served if pastoral counselors engage clients as the primary agents of change, who actively use whatever is available to them—a counselor, a friend, a congregational leader, or a book. Thinking of pastoral counselors and clients as partners in therapy suggests greater use of therapies that reduce the hierarchy between client and counselor and that privilege the client's self-knowledge, indigenous resources, and motivation. Therapies that highlight the counselor's specialized knowledge or her or his privileged position in diagnosis, or suggest that a therapist understands the client's life better than the client may undermine motivation, derail client internal resources, or encourage client passivity.

Pastoral counselors may also need to examine their assumptions and expectations about change. Many research respondents revealed that they were opposed to short-term therapy or counseling that focused on behavior change. This was seen as "Band-Aid" therapy with little lasting value. "True change" requires extensive time in therapy and is marked by personality transformation. One pastoral counselor stated that his determination to "stick with" long-term transformation instead of facilitating the shorter-term change requested by clients was a form of grace. These assumptions may disempower otherwise motivated clients by insisting that successful therapy requires them to join the therapist's assumptive world. Studies consistently show that most people, including clients, are capable of relatively rapid change that endures. A small number of clients (less than 25 percent) appear to benefit significantly from extended periods of therapy.[25] Most clients stay in counseling, with or without their therapist's approval, for an average of eight sessions. The most frequent number of therapy visits is one. Pastoral counselors have often interpreted these short-term interchanges as failure. However, evidence suggests that clients often did not return because they felt better. Taking action to see a therapist stimulated them to make important changes in their lives, or they got what they wanted from the therapist in one or a few sessions. Many clients are unwilling to tell their counselors they are no longer needed and so simply drop from sight. These observations suggest that pastoral counselors could improve client-therapist partnerships by using active learning and interactional therapies, extratherapy resources such as self-help materials,[26] and careful attention to what clients say about their own improvement. Howard Stone has provided an excellent model for short-term pastoral counseling that takes client-counselor collaboration seriously and makes the most of client resources.[27] Xolani Kacela has proposed a one-session model for pastoral counseling that seeks to mobilize client resources and self-healing.[28]

Faith and Mental Health

Interviews (WPC) indicated that pastoral counselors may overestimate their contribution to therapy by focusing on pastoral identity and relational and therapeutic skills while underestimating the power their clients hold as the primary agents of change. On the other hand, pastoral counselors were highly attuned to client resources that are overlooked by other kinds of counselors. They tended to be keen observers of clients' spiritual resources, religious connections, and longing for spiritual and personal growth. Most also stated that, though their own spiritual commitments were central to their pastoral identity, they relied almost exclusively on the *client's* religious expression, religious heritage, and sense of spirituality. Here, instead of being the authority, pastoral counselors turned to clients' self-knowledge and personal authority. Clients were drawn into active discussion and reflection, and at times prayed or read scripture with their therapists. These activities benefit clients at two levels. First, active engagement mobilizes the client's self-healing abilities and may act as a corrective for more passive approaches to therapy. Second, research in faith and mental health shows that there are direct benefits to incorporating religious and spiritual factors into therapy.

Research[29] shows that religious involvement, personal faith, and spirituality have positive effects. It appears that a large majority of people turn to religious resources to cope with life stress, personal loss, natural disaster, war, mental and physical illness, and other problems in living. One analysis of more than one hundred studies in religion and mental health showed a consistent statistically significant relationship between religious involvement and life satisfaction, happiness, positive mood, and high morale.[30] These results appear to hold across international, cultural, and world religious boundaries[31] (with the exception of Northern Europe).[32] Though the vast majority of studies note that religion and spirituality have benefits for mental health, there are exceptions. Beliefs that encourage destructive or punitive images of God, aggression, prejudice and discrimination, physical abuse, domination over others, dogmatic or obsessive thinking, perfectionism, or dependency tend to have negative effects on psychological well-being. Some individuals who are trying unsuccessfully to believe, or who believe differently from friends or family, may experience more stress and less life satisfaction. In general, however, personal spirituality and religiosity are associated with a lower incidence of mental disorder, fewer self-destructive behaviors, less anxiety, less depression, and faster recovery from depression. Clinical trials show religious interventions produce faster results in reducing clinical mental health symptoms than therapies that exclude them. Religion may be particularly helpful for persons with severe or persistent mental illnesses. Koenig suggests religion and spirituality can benefit therapy by

- Promoting a positive worldview,
- Helping clients make sense of difficult situations,
- Providing purpose and meaning,
- Discouraging maladaptive coping,
- Enhancing social support,
- Promoting other-directedness,
- Helping clients release the need for personal control in uncontrollable situations,
- Helping clients with appropriate forgiveness,
- Encouraging thankfulness, and
- Encouraging hope.[33]

Pastoral counselors excel in identifying and mobilizing clients toward spiritually based self-healing in three ways: (1) they are highly attuned to listen for spiritual meanings in therapy and bring these into conversations; (2) they help clients evaluate "when religion gets sick"[34] and is detrimental to mental health or coping; and (3) they value the process of personal growth and spiritual discovery. This last dimension may account for much of pastoral counselors' overall bias toward long-term therapy. Analysis of data (WPC) suggests that pastoral counselors often make no distinction between psychotherapeutic change and spiritual growth and discovery. For many, long-term psychotherapy appeared to function as a form of spiritual direction, with a goal of spiritual transformation rather than symptom relief or reduction. In many cases pastoral counselors used a hybrid therapeutic language that communicated spiritual values but used psychodynamic terminology to anchor their work and distinguish themselves from spiritual directors. Most indicated that they were "less directive" than spiritual directors but anticipated many of the same outcomes: mobilizing spiritual resources for client coping, experiencing personal transformation, having an improved relationship with God, and developing "spiritually grounded" ways of being in relationship with self and others. Pastoral counselors expected that "addressing the spiritual dimension" would engender hope and stimulate the client toward personal transformation.

Mobilizing Client Hope in Counseling

"Pastoral counseling provides an avenue of grace and hope" was a common statement in pastoral counselor interviews. Hope almost always referred to relief from suffering and "expectation of personal transformation"; in other words, to change what can be changed and survive what cannot be changed with integrity and a vision for the future. This is consistent with Frank's observation that effective psychotherapy combats demoralization by persuading clients to transform pathogenic meanings to ones that rekindle hope, enhance mastery, heighten self-esteem, and reintegrate clients into their social groups. For pastoral counselors, though, *hope* was a term with deeply religious and spiritual roots. For Christian pastoral counselors it is anchored in the trajectory of Judeo-Christian history and the story of God's universal, all-inclusive love that survives sin, tragedy, and evil in order to restore that which has been lost. Hope is God's relationship to the world. It lures all creation toward fulfillment. Through the symbol of Jesus and the cross, God stands in solidarity with wounded humanity and embodies the promise that sin, evil, and tragedy will not overwhelm history or render individual suffering meaningless. Instead, the cross transforms suffering into life-sustaining meanings and a vision for the future. Transforming paradigms of hope are present in all religious and spiritual traditions of healing. Pastoral counselors can offer multiple avenues to hope by bringing together psychotherapeutic explanatory myths and healing rituals with those from religious and spiritual traditions. This may be particularly important for demoralized people who cannot see hope in their life circumstances.

Recent research helps pastoral counselors better understand how hope works in the therapy process. One group of studies suggests that hope is emotion based—it rises and falls on emotional reaction to events. A more recent group of studies identifies central cognitive processes that determine the ability to hope and explain interruptions in hope. In order to hope, individuals need both successful *pathway* thinking and successful *agency* thinking.[35] Pathway thinking takes place when a client cognitively constructs a possible route to change or to a different experience. Agency thinking takes place when a client finds a way to start toward or continue toward a goal. Both must be present for hope. Research also suggests that facilitating these two dimensions of hope is critical in the early stages of therapy since the most substantial part of change takes place in the first few weeks of counseling. Both pathway and agency hope are stimulated as therapists help clients set goals and manage emotional factors that keep them from envisioning goals or taking action toward goals.

Though pastoral counselors use the same therapeutic settings, theories (believable myths), and technical procedures (rituals) as other therapists, they provide two additional symbolic avenues of hope not available to other therapists. When pastoral counselors bring the notion of pastoral presence to sessions, they express a transcendent hope that God is active and present in counseling sessions. They also bring a rich tradition of spiritual stories, religious ritual, and communal connections. These expand hope beyond the temporal facts of a client's demoralization, can stimulate new pathway and agency thinking, and can suggest extratherapeutic sources to support hope and change. Interviews (WPC) showed that pastoral counselors often stepped out of psychological paradigms with clients and into the language and practices of faith, spirituality, and religious belief. Many used religious stories or scripture. Some prayed with clients, asked clients to pray or journal outside session, had theological discussions with clients, referred clients to religious services, or performed religious rituals as part of therapy.[36] In nearly every case, pastoral counselors' purpose could be interpreted as stimulating pathway thinking or agency thinking, or managing emotional factors blocking hope. Production of hope may be one of pastoral counselors' most distinguishing features.

Fifteen Percent Factor: Pastoral Counseling Skills and Theories of Therapy

In 1952, more than fifty years after the development of psychoanalysis, Hans Eysenck[37] reviewed more than eight thousand cases and concluded there was no evidence that psychotherapy ("Freudian or otherwise") had any effect on the outcome of psychological problems. He concluded that people spontaneously recovered from psychological problems at about the same rate as those who received treatment. Clinicians' strong *belief* that therapy was effective did not make it so. Eysenck's critique stimulated an avalanche of research over the following fifty years that left little doubt that psychotherapy is beneficial. People who receive psychotherapy for psychological and other problems in living fare better than those who do not. One large meta-analytic study showed that by the end of treatment, the average person receiving psychotherapy was better off than 80 percent of people with the same problem who did not receive treatment.[38] However, despite claims of charismatic leaders and clinicians' deep beliefs, this research also failed to show that any single model of therapy has any advantage over others. (One exception may be very limited empirically validated techniques for specific disorders.)[39] While treatment models do not determine outcome, they provide the myths that influence how relationships are structured and what rituals are helpful. In the following illustrative case study, notice how different myths (or theories) shape two counselors' relationship and procedures with the same client:

Gregory T. is a pastoral counselor employed by a counseling center in a metropolitan hospital. He claims as his guiding theory object relations therapy with careful attention to neuropsychology. His new client, Eric P., was referred by his physician. Before Gregory met Eric, the receptionist handed him a clipboard with several forms that summarized Eric's personal history, medical history, medical insurance information, and a brief description and history of the problem for which he had been referred. At the end of the first session, Gregory wrote an assessment narrative that described Eric and his personal history as it relates to the problem presented. He also documented that he arrived at a preliminary diagnosis of adjustment disorder with depressed mood using the DSM-IV-TR, that he has discussed this with his client, and that he and his client have agreed to a course of treatment. The report ends with a description of how therapy will proceed.

Eric saw his physician because he was not sleeping well, was irritable with his family, and was unreasonably fearful of losing the job to which he had just been promoted. After ruling out physical problems, his physician concluded that he might be experiencing "psycho-physiological responses to stress" and referred him to the pastoral counseling clinic. When Eric arrived for his appointment, he was met at a glass window by a receptionist with a package of forms for him to fill out. He found Gregory to be professional and competent. Gregory listened carefully to him and took his symptoms seriously. Near the end of the session, Gregory summarized what Eric had told him, recounted his environmental pressures and his emotional reactions to them. He was relieved when Gregory stated that he was "mildly depressed" by recent stressors in his life. Gregory informed him that this diagnosis would go on his insurance forms if he agreed to it. Eric and Gregory talked about the meaning of the diagnosis and how treatment would proceed. They agreed to weekly sessions in which Eric would talk about those things important to him. Together they would discover ways for him to feel more competent and manage his depression.

Linda R. is a pastoral counselor in private practice. She describes her approach to therapy as feminist and collaborative. Her new client, Eric, was referred by his minister because he was not sleeping, was irritable with his family, and was unreasonably fearful about losing the job to which he had just been promoted. When Eric arrived for his session, Linda met him in the reception area, gave him a clipboard with a client data form, a client-therapist disclosure form, and an informed consent document to sign. When he was finished reading and signing, Linda invited him to her office. During the session she asked many questions about Eric, his family, and the pressures of his job. She avoided assumptions and "reading" Eric's feelings or motives. She also avoided diagnostic and technical language that might mystify the problem or create a worse problem by pathologizing Eric's experience. Linda also made sure that Eric stayed the expert about his own life. She used his words and expressions as much as possible. Together they defined Eric's difficulty as "worrying about losing what he had gained" and "feeling sad" when he thought of that. She explored with him what was different about those times he felt fearful or sad and those times when he did not. Linda wondered with Eric about the relational effects of cultural demands that he must succeed financially to be a good man and husband. Near the end of the session Linda asked Eric what he found helpful about their conversation and how it could have been more meaningful. Eric suggested he would like to invite his wife, Sylvia, into the sessions. She was his best friend and a "stakeholder" in this problem. Linda believed that expanding the therapy system would provide a broader perspective and more options. They agreed to meet the following week with Sylvia as a therapy partner.

Eric felt good about his first session with Linda. He had been worried that he was developing a mental illness and was relieved when she made no diagnosis. Instead, she had used language that made him feel his was a "normal" problem. He was "stuck" instead of sick. Also, it wasn't just his problem—it was also part of a bigger picture about how men were stressed by patriarchal culture. Linda's "wondering" questions were particularly meaningful. They made him feel that he shared control of the session. At the same time, Linda had a way of wording her questions and responses that made him think in a new way. His decision to ask Sylvia into the session was part of his own "wondering" about what would help.

As the cases above indicate, counselors' approaches to therapy may differ and produce the same results. Frank's work shows that all effective therapy provides the same thing: an emotionally charged, confiding relationship with a therapist; a therapeutic setting; a guiding myth or conceptual scheme that provides an explanation for symptoms and a rationale for treatment; and a ritual that requires active participation of both client and therapist. Psychotherapeutic theories and models—of which there are now hundreds—structure these four elements. What appears to be important is consensus between the therapist's guiding myth, the client's assumptive world, and the social context in which counseling takes place. No single therapy model provides this for all clients. Instead of organizing their practice around one primary theoretical commitment, pastoral counselors need to be flexible enough to accommodate a variety of client assumptive worlds and social contexts and wise enough to refer when client-therapist consensus is unlikely.

One area of growth for the field will be to examine the many ways that *clients* present to therapy, the variety of their assumptive worlds, and the different ways they balance cognitive, emotional, interactional, and behavioral values. This information can help pastoral counselors identify blind spots created by a single domi-nant theory. It can also lead pastoral counselors toward quality training in alternative models that will meet the needs of clients who otherwise would not seek or benefit from pastoral counseling. Pastoral counselors are highly attuned to emotion-based therapies that may not match all, or perhaps even most, client assumptive worlds. Careful integration of cognitive and behavioral therapies, along with interactional therapies such as strategic, solution-focused, narrative, and collaborative therapies, can expand this foundation. Pastoral counselors and clients will also benefit from attention to empirically supported treatments for very specific problems (such as phobias or anorexia) as these emerge in the psy-chotherapy literature. Diversification of counseling theory is important for clients and for the field of pastoral counseling. At the same time, this must be a critical theological process. No psy-chotherapy model is adequate for pastoral counseling. All high-light particular dimensions of human life, relationships, and personality and fail to reflect the fullness and diversity of human life. Pastoral counselors must examine theologically the meaning systems, worldviews, and vision of human life expressed by coun-seling theories before integrating them into their identity and work.

If pastoral counselors risk limitation by committing to single the-ories, they have much to offer in the realm of spiritual and reli-giously grounded myths and rituals. In interviews, pastoral counselors often referred to the way they created a context in ther-apy that supported a client's creative use of spiritual material and religious ritual. More than half reported that they prayed with their clients under very specific conditions that required careful thought, preparation, and interpretation in the context of counsel-ing. Most counselors believed this helped mobilize clients' spiritual resources. Counselors in religiously conservative and evangelical traditions sometimes prayed routinely with clients because it was part of the client's assumptive world and helped frame therapy as a place to expect change. Pastoral counselors also incorporated Scripture[40] into the ritual of therapy by framing interventions and interpretations in the context of familiar biblical stories. Many reported using faith language, such as grace, salvation, or libera-tion, as part of a myth/belief system to understand problems and possible solutions. Pastoral counselors were almost universal in claiming that faith resources were used only after careful assessment of the client's assumptive world and after they had established a context-specific consensus about how spiritual resources related to the counseling process.

Pastoral Counseling, Timing, and Goals

Pastoral counselors regard their work as successful when clients (1) change what they can to improve their spiritual, emotional, or relational life, or (2) change their attitudes when other improvements are impossible. This, in Frank's paradigm, overcomes demoralization. However, not all clients appear to change, which can frustrate both clients and counselors. By understanding change as a process that moves through several stages, pastoral counselors can help clients set appropriate goals, reduce demoralization when clients get stuck, and provide a more realistic assessment of client progress.

Prochaska's[41] thirty-year examination of human change reveals that it is a process that unfolds over time through six stages: pre-contemplation, contemplation, preparation, action, maintenance, and termination. Unlike other stage theories, there is no biological or other inherent motivation for people to move from one stage of change to another. However, developmental events (reaching adulthood or middle age) and environmental events (making a geographic move or facing a job loss) can motivate people toward change. His analysis suggests that most people coming for counseling are split between the first three stages of change. About 40 percent are "pre-contemplators." These individuals are not seriously considering change. They often go to therapy because a spouse, parent, employer, or friend has insisted that they seek help or are bothered by their feelings or behavior. They may have tried to change but have been unsuccessful. Many are demoralized. People in this stage may avoid thinking about their problems and may be seen as "in denial," as resistant, or as unmotivated clients. By identifying clients who are pre-contemplators, pastoral counselors may be able to form effective relationships, set appropriate goals, and see therapeutic gains with clients who otherwise would not gain from counseling. Counselors working with these clients would avoid direct behavioral or emotional change and focus instead on short-term examination of the pros and cons of change. Therapy in this stage would be successful if clients began to explore pros and cons or found enough pros to enter the contemplation stage. Clients who make this shift often become more conscious of how their problem affects their emotions, behavior, or relationships. They may experience a dramatic sense of relief and a sense of hope. Doing this can help them engage in therapy, though they may not be ready for rituals of change or an intense therapeutic relationship.

Another 40 percent of those seeking counseling will be in the contemplation stage of change. In this stage, people have short-term goals to change but are highly aware of how much change costs. Therapists may view these clients as chronic procrastinators or help-rejecting complainers. The appropriate goal for these clients is to reduce the cons that keep them from entering the action stage. This might include self-examination, evaluating relationships carefully, anticipating positive outcomes, or looking for exceptions to the cons. Counseling in this stage may be both supportive and confrontive.

Only about 20 percent of clients who see a counselor are in the preparation stage of change. These individuals have usually made a commitment to change and are ready to engage their therapists to mobilize self-healing resources. They are ready for action and often delight their therapists. People moving from contemplation to action may experience feelings of liberation as pros begin to outweigh the cons for change. The appropriate goal for the preparation stage is to help clients evaluate needed changes, plumb the emotional, relational, and spiritual depths of their ambivalence about change, and begin working to set concrete goals that can be achieved.

In the action stage clients have made (or are making) changes in their lives but must work to assure changes are long lasting and transformative. In this stage pastoral counselors and clients can agree upon an explanatory myth and actively engage in rituals to mobilize self-healing. Therapy helps clients reach specific goals and manage the contingencies that undermine progress. During this stage, clients will move toward goals, work through setbacks with their therapist, wonder if the work is worth it, resist change at times, and exercise both pathway and agency hope. Demoralization improves as clients make discernable progress toward their goals. The action stage demands that pastoral counselors help clients assess changes they are making, begin to evaluate themselves in more positive ways, and integrate changes into the breadth of their cognitive, emotional, spiritual, social, and behavioral life.

In the maintenance stage, clients and therapists work together to prevent relapses by preparing for the pressures that undermine change. Termination represents successful change by a client who has developed resources to self-maintain gains.

Organizing Therapy

Instead of describing how counselors organize therapy, the following case study illustrates how the ideas and practices described in this chapter would translate into the work of therapy.

John and Deborah were referred to Denise M. for marital therapy. The couple have been married for ten years. They have two children, Keisha, age five, and DeWayne, three. Deborah made the appointment for counseling after a particularly painful marital argument.

Denise has been a pastoral counselor for fifteen years. She was trained as a psychodynamic therapist. For more than a decade she worked almost exclusively with individuals. When she did accept a couple in therapy, one spouse often dropped out, and she worked with the one who remained, often toward divorce. Denise was uncomfortable with this pattern but increasingly received referrals for marital counseling from local pastors. She concluded that her primary therapy model (guiding myth) worked well with individual clients but did not feel it was adequate to guide her work with both partners in a coupled relationship. She was unsure whether this was a failure of technique, her use of technique, or the guiding myth itself. For more than a year she read about research in couples therapy and attended workshops in John Gottman's model of marital therapy[42] and emotionally focused couples therapy.[43] She was drawn to emotionally focused therapy's concentration on adult attachment but also saw that Gottman's behavioral model offered a rich source of assessment tools, a way of identifying destructive behaviors in conflict, and a set of intervention techniques that were very helpful to couples she saw. She contracted a supervisor and began to accept more couples for counseling.

As a pastoral counselor, Denise was concerned about the assumptive worlds and visions of human life and relationship expressed by these new models. She initiated several theological conversations with colleagues that helped her think through implicit values and theological anthropologies contained in both theories. She concluded that both had much to offer. Both were generally consistent with her own beliefs about human life and coupled relationships. However, both also challenged her to rethink her assumptions about change and "healing." Neither theory looked toward personality transformation or relied on diagnosis of individual pathology. Both were shorter term and expected that relationship change could take place without long-term personal insight. Both transferred emphasis away from individual client concerns and saw couple interaction as the "client." In conversation with her supervisor, she began to construct a way of working with couples that included elements of both models of therapy and that incorporated couple spirituality.[44]

When Denise saw John and Deborah, she listened carefully to each. She was aware that pastoral presence in this counseling context meant that she had to engage both John and Deborah as individuals and the couple as an entity in its own right. In the first session she balanced listening and responding to both. She soon realized that John was attuned to emotionally toned empathy while Deborah seemed impatient with emotionally toned responses. She was more concerned that Denise "understand" her "position" and give her concrete things to do to change "the situation." Denise worked hard to respond to John with emotionally toned responses and to Deborah with cognitive understanding. She focused the session on the couple by asking them to talk together in her office about a problem they could not resolve. This allowed her to observe the couple's pattern of conflict interaction and focus the couple relationship as the unit of treatment. She also gave the couple self-report assessment inventories to fill out at home that would help her assess where each was in the marriage, define areas of conflict, and help identify internal emotional models that motivated each in the relationship. The second session, Denise met with each separately to assess for spouse abuse and comorbidity,[45] *and to get a better sense of John and Deborah as individuals. By the end of the third session, Denise had established a contract for counseling with three goals: strengthen the couple's marital friendship, develop the couple's capacity to have a marital argument and still feel positive about each other, and agree on how housework and child care chores would be divided between John and Deborah.*

At the end of the fifth session, Denise reviewed her work with her supervisor. She believed she had established a working therapeutic relationship with the couple. She described her relationship as pastoral presence "stretched in three ways": She "felt with" John as he learned to hear his wife's dissatisfaction without stonewalling in session. She actively engaged Deborah's complaints and thought with her about how these expressed fear that she was losing her husband. She used homework and in-session assignments to help the couple engage, coach them toward managing relational gridlock, and practice new ways to repair marital fights. She worked particularly hard to assess the couple's strengths and community, spiritual, and family resources. Both were motivated to improve their relationship. Neither wanted a divorce. The couple were active in church and had good support for their relationship within that community. Both were religiously committed. Both had benevolent images of God and a sense that God wanted them to succeed. On the other hand, Denise observed that John had difficulty with both pathway and agency hope. He "wished" that things could be different. He could envision things as better but could not imagine what he could do to reach that goal.

Denise also evaluated the couple's position in the cycle of change. John was contemplating change. Deborah was in the preparation stage of change. To move into the action stage, John would need to improve his ability to hope. Both John and Deborah would have to examine the costs of change and decide if the pros outweighed the cons. Denise decided to use two interventions. First, she used Gottman's Dreams-Within-Conflict[46] intervention to strengthen John's pathway thinking (hope). She also used exception questions (narrative therapy and solution-focused therapy) to help him identify ways he was already using pathway thinking to imagine reaching some goals. This intervention also helped both John and Deborah identify unmet attachment needs. Her second intervention was to help John and Deborah identify secondary reactive patterns (emotionally focused therapy) that undermined hope that each had for secure marital attachment. She found Gottman's Four Horsemen of the Apocalypse[47] very useful to help the couple identify these repetitive, destructive interchanges. As religious people, the couple found the Four Horsemen image amusing but also quickly engaged it as a powerful metaphor for them. Denise frequently used the image of "God's grace" to affirm the couple as they softened toward each other and engaged in new, nonreactive ways. "Faithfulness" was a metaphor she used to describe John and Deborah's commitment to work together toward a better marriage. John referred to improvements as "God's redemption." He began to find new pathways for hope in these images. He also tended to shift responsibility for agency onto God.

Denise's plan for the next few sessions was to continue helping the couple manage and repair conflicts, and to design homework assignments that interrupted negative secondary reactions and encouraged emotional vulnerability with each other. Denise expected that these interventions would stimulate the couple to identify and more seriously consider the pros and cons of change.

Notes

1. Howard Stone, "The Congregational Setting of Pastoral Counseling: A Study of Pastoral Counseling Theorists from 1949–1999," *Journal of Pastoral Care* 55, no. 2 (2001): 187.

2. T. B. Karasu, "The Specificity versus Nonspecificity Dilemma: Toward Identifying Therapeutic Change Agents," *American Journal of Psychiatry* 143 (1986).

3. For example, S. L. Garfield and A. E. Bergin, "Introduction and Historical Overview," in *Handbook of Psychotherapy and Behavior Change,* eds. A. E. Bergin and S. L. Garfield (New York: Wiley, 1994); J. C. Norcross and C. F. Newman, "Psychotherapy Integration: Setting the Context," in *Handbook of Psychotherapy Integration,* eds. J. C. Norcross and M. R. Goldfried (New York: Basic Books, 1992).

4. One group of studies found that about 50 percent of clients show clinically significant change in 8 to 10 sessions and 75 percent of clients show clinically significant results within 26 sessions. See S. W. Kadera, M. J. Lambert, and A. A. Andrews, "How Much Therapy Is Really Enough: A Session-by-Session Analysis of the Psychotherapy Dose-Effect Relationship," *Journal of Psychotherapy: Practice and Research* 5 (1996); K. I. Howard, S. M. Kopta, M. S. Krause, and D. E. Orlinsky, "The Dose-Effective Relationship in Psychotherapy," *American Psychologist* 41 (1986).

5. Jerome D. Frank, *Persuasion and Healing: A Comparative Study of Psychotherapy* (Baltimore: Johns Hopkins University Press, 1961).

6. This raises a problem: "Psychiatric diagnoses may conceal culturally influenced covert judgments about whether the person's behavior is pathological and whether the source of that behavior lies in the person or in the culture." Jerome D. Frank and Julia B. Frank, *Persuasion and Healing: A Comparative Study of Psychotherapy,* 3rd ed. (Baltimore: Johns Hopkins University Press, 1991), 8.

7. Ibid., 14.

8. Ibid., 52.

9. M. J. Lambert, "Implications of Outcome Research for Psychotherapy

Integration," in *Handbook of Psychotherapy Integration*, eds. J. C. Norcross and M. R. Goldfried (New York: Basic Books, 1992).

10. M. A. Hubble, B. L. Duncan, and S. D. Miller, eds., *The Heart and Soul of Change: What Works in Therapy* (Washington, D. C.: American Psychological Association, 1999).

11. Heinz Kohut, *How Does Analysis Cure?* eds. Arnold Goldberg and Paul Stapansky (Chicago: University of Chicago Press, 1984).

12. Alexandra Bachelor, "How Clients Perceive Therapist Empathy: A Content Analysis of 'Received' Empathy," *Psychotherapy: Theory and Practice* 25 (1988), 227–40; Alexandra Bachelor, "Clients Perception of the Therapeutic Alliance: A Qualitative Analysis," *Journal of Counseling Psychology* 42 (3) (1995), 323–38.

13. Alexandra Bachelor and Adam Horvath, "The Therapeutic Relationship," in *The Heart and Soul of Change: What Works in Therapy*, eds. M. A. Hubble, B. L. Duncan, and S. D. Miller (Washington, D.C.: American Psychological Association, 1999), 145.

14. Harlene Anderson and Diane Gehart, *Collaborative Therapy: Relationships and Conversations That Make a Difference* (New York: Routledge, 2007).

15. Sylvia London and Florence Rosenberg, "Migracion Y Cultura: Implicaciones Para La Practica Terapeutica," in *Terapias Postmodernas: Aportaciones Construccionistas*, ed. Gilberto Limon Arce (Mexico City: Editorial Pax Mexico, 2005).

16. Lee H. Butler, *Liberating Our Dignity, Saving Our Souls* (St. Louis: Chalice Press, 2006).

17. Bachelor and Horvath, "The Therapeutic Relationship," 140.

18. L. M. Najavits and H. H. Strupp, "Differences in the Effectiveness of Psychodynamic Therapists: A Process-Outcome Study," *Psychotherapy* 31 (1994); Bachelor and Horvath, "The Therapeutic Relationship."

19. Frank and Frank, *Persuasion and Healing: A Comparative Study of Psychotherapy*; Harold Koenig, *Faith and Mental Health: Religious Resources for Healing* (West Conshohocken, Pa.: Templeton Foundation Press, 2005).

20. A. Klineman, *Rethinking Psychiatry: From Cultural Category to Personal Experience* (New York: Free Press), 112, as cited by D. E. Orlinsky, K. Grawe, and B. K. Parks, "Process and Outcome in Psychotherapy—Noch Einmal," in *Handbook of Psychotherapy and Behavior Change*, 4th ed., eds. A. E. Bergin and S. L. Garfield (New York: Wiley, 1994), 278.

21. J. O. Prochaska, C. C. DiClemente, and J. C. Norcross, *Changing for Good* (New York: Morrow, 1994).

22. Karen Tallman and Arthur C. Bohart, "The Client as a Common Factor: Clients as Self-Healers," in *The Heart and Soul of Change: What Works in Therapy*, eds. M. A. Hubble, B. L. Duncan, and S. D. Miller (Washington, D.C.: American Psychological Association, 1999).

23. Najavits and Strupp, "Differences in the Effectiveness of Psychodynamic Therapists: A Process-Outcome Study"; D. L. Rennie, "Toward a Representation of the Client's Experience of the Psychotherapeutic Hour," in *Client-Centered and Experiential Psychotherapy in the Nineties*, eds. G. Lietaer, J. Rombauts, and R. van Balen (1990); Tallman and Bohart, "The Client as a Common Factor: Clients as Self-Healers."

24. R. Elliot and E. James, "Varieties of Client Experience in Psychotherapy: An Analysis of the Literature," *Clinical Psychology Review* 9 (1989).

25. Howard, Kopta, Krause, and Orlinsky, "The Dose-Effective Relationship in Psychotherapy"; Kadera, Lambert, and Andrews, "How Much Therapy Is Really Enough: A Session-by-Session Analysis of the Psychotherapy Dose-Effect Relationship."

26. Large meta-analytic studies show that self-help resources are as effective for a wide range of problems as interventions with a therapist. See R. A. Gould and G. A. Clum, "A Meta-Analysis of Self-Help Treatment Approaches," *Clinical Psychology Review* 13 (1993); F. Scoggin et al., "Efficacy of Self-Administered Treatment Programs: Meta-Analytical Review," *Professional Psychology: Research and Practice* 21 (1990).

27. Howard W. Stone, *Strategies for Brief Pastoral Counseling,* ed. Howard W. Stone (Minneapolis: Fortress Press, 2001).

28. Xolani Kacela, "One Session Is Enough: Pastoral Counseling for African American Families," *American Journal of Pastoral Counseling* 6, no. 3 (2003).

29. H. Koenig, ed., *Handbook of Religion and Mental Health* (San Diego: Academic Press, 1998); H. Koenig, M. McCullough, and D. Larson, *Handbook of Religion and Health* (New York: Oxford University Press, 2001); Koenig, *Faith and Mental Health: Religious Resources for Healing.*

30. Koenig, *Faith and Mental Health: Religious Resources for Healing.*

31. L. J. Francis and P. Kaldor, "The Relationship between Psychological Well-Being and Christian Faith and Practice in an Australian Population Sample," *Journal for the Scientific Study of Religion* 41, no. 1 (2002); J. Hintikka et al., "Religious Attendance and Life Satisfaction in the Finnish General Population," *Journal of Psychology and Theology* 29, no. 2 (2001); Koenig, *Faith and Mental Health: Religious Resources for Healing.*

32. Northern Europe was an exception, possibly because so few people claim that religious faith is significant to their lives.

33. Koenig, *Faith and Mental Health: Religious Resources for Healing,* 134–40.

34. W. E. Oates, *When Religion Gets Sick* (Philadelphia: Westminster Press, 1970).

35. C. R. Snyder, *The Psychology of Hope: You Can Get There from Here* (New York: Free Press, 1994); C. R. Snyder, S. T. Michael, and J. S. Cheavens, "Hope as a Psychotherapeutic Foundation of Common Factors, Placebos, and Expectancies," in *The Heart and Soul of Change: What Works in Therapy.*

36. Rituals were used very rarely. Pastoral counselors interviewed stated that they must have an "extremely good reason" to perform a ritual such as Communion or a healing rite, that these rituals required careful preparation with the client, and that careful follow-up is necessary since the outcome of a ritual is unknown.

37. H. J. Eysenck, "The Effects of Psychotherapy: An Evaluation," *Journal of Consulting Psychology* 16 (1952).

38. M. L. Smith, G. V. Glass, and T. I. Miller, *The Benefits of Psychotherapy* (Baltimore: Johns Hopkins University Press, 1980).

39. Examples include emotionally focused couples therapy, behavior therapy for headache, cognitive behavior therapy for chronic pain, systematic desensitiza-

tion for simple phobia, interpersonal therapy for bulimia, etc. (American Psychological Association, Division 12, Update on Empirically Validated Therapies, http://www.apa.org/divisions/Div12/est/newrpt.pdf). There is considerable debate about whether this research shows actual differences in treatment outcome or simply privileges some techniques over others by making them the focus of a research agenda.

40. For a particularly sensitive treatment of prayer and Scripture in pastoral care and counseling, see Edward P. Wimberly, *Pastoral Counseling and Spiritual Values: A Black Point of View* (Nashville: Abingdon Press, 1982); Edward P. Wimberly, *Prayer in Pastoral Counseling: Suffering, Healing, and Discernment* (Louisville: Westminster John Knox Press, 1990); Edward P. Wimberly, *Using Scripture in Pastoral Counseling* (Nashville: Abingdon Press, 1994).

41. J. O. Prochaska, *Systems of Psychotherapy: A Transtheoretical Analysis* (Chicago: Dorsey Press, 1979); J. O. Prochaska and C. C. DiClemente, "Transtheoretical Therapy: Toward a More Integrative Model of Change," *Psychotherapy: Theory, Research, and Practice* 19 (1982); Prochaska, DiClemente, and Norcross, *Changing for Good.*

42. John Gottman, *The Marriage Clinic: A Scientifically Based Marital Therapy* (New York: Norton, 1999).

43. Susan Johnson, *The Practice of Emotionally Focused Marital Therapy: Creating Connection* (New York: Brunner-Mazel, 1996).

44. For example, Mary Oliver, *Conjugal Spirituality: The Primacy of Mutual Love in Christian Tradition* (Kansas City, Mo.: Sheed and Ward, 1994).

45. *Comorbidity* refers to two or more problems existing at one time. For instance, a couple's problem can be complicated by an individual's depression, substance abuse, chaotic lifestyle, or an affair.

46. Gottman, *The Marriage Clinic: A Scientifically-Based Marital Therapy.*

47. Ibid. *Four Horsemen of the Apocalypse* refers to four positions that couples take in conflict: criticism, defensiveness, contempt, and stonewalling.

CHAPTER 6

Thinking Theologically and Ethically

Theological Reflection

Pastoral counselors reflect theologically and ethically on their work. Almost every pastoral counselor interviewed (WPC) reported that "theological reflection" was an important component of their work. This meant several things: "I reflect theologically on my work with clients"; "I think about my own spiritual life in relationship to my counseling work"; or "I think about how I integrate spirituality into what I do in therapy." In most cases, pastoral counselors felt unprepared to describe exactly how they did "theological reflection" or "spiritual reflection," but they were clear that it influenced work with clients. "I do it, but I have a hard time explaining how I do it" was a common response. Only a few could name a method of reflection or the theological frame from which their reflective practices were drawn. As noted in chapter 4, most counselors modeled influential supervisors. Pastoral counselors expect theological, or spiritual, reflection to accomplish at least five ends:

- To gain insight into one's own thoughts, feelings, spiritual understanding, or theological positions in relationship to experience with a client or colleague;
- To gain insight into a client's religious or emotional world and relationships with God, family, or community;
- To assess and guide therapist goals and interactions with clients;

- To make decisions about appropriate use of therapy models or techniques;
- To assess client progress and growth.

These have a common theme. Theological reflection is about therapist discernment. It is expected to produce several kinds of knowledge—cognitive data, emotional insight, spiritual wisdom, sociocultural comprehension, and relational awareness. These are the building blocks of discernment that guide pastoral counselors. Though few counselors felt competent to name or describe their reflective method, most recalled specific experiences in which they knew (sometimes afterward) that they had reflected theologically. Analysis of these experiences revealed several reflective motifs.[1]

Reflective Motifs

The most common motif is anchored in pastoral counselor formation. In this motif, reflection is not so much a conscious, reflective activity as it is an internalized function of identity gained in formation. It is often learned by the counselor (or supervisor who influenced the counselor) in CPE. This form of reflection emphasizes incarnational pastoral presence over critical cognitive-reflective processes. Discernment is guided by emotional and conceptual maps internalized through supervision and personal formation. These maps provide an aesthetic sense of pattern and metaphor deeply connected to the pastoral counselor's identity and value system. Reflection is an intuitive process. It relies on empathic pastoral presence and takes place in the immediacy of a session when a counselor recognizes emotional, relational, or behavioral similarities between a particular counseling situation and a dominant religious metaphor, spiritual principle, or biblical narrative. This intuitive discernment produces therapeutic metaphors that help organize pastoral presence in transforming ways. The strength of this motif is its immediate access to religious and spiritual information embedded in the person of the counselor and its relational power in therapy. It also holds liabilities. First, it assumes that the therapist has special knowledge gained through clinical training. This establishes a hierarchy and power differential in therapy that may encourage the therapist to value his or her internalized value system and aesthetic maps over clients' perceptions, values, and voices. Second, when theological reflection is an internal, intuitive process of the pastoral counselor, it can become disconnected from faith communities. Counselors then risk isolation and noncritical individualism, and may mistake countertransference for reflection.

A second set of motifs expresses a correlational method. Correlational approaches to integrating behavioral sciences and theology were discussed in chapter 4. To summarize briefly, correlation motifs rest on the assumption that there is a meaningful relationship between theological knowledge and common human experience.[2] Knowledge from one source can be correlated and compared with the other. By comparing theological knowledge with experiences in psychotherapy, both sources of information are valued, can be expanded, and can be protected from theological, therapeutic, and theoretical myopia. Reflection is an active, cognitive, and critical practice. It is meant to sharpen a pastoral counselor's view of a case, refine assessment, and provide options for treatment strategies. As mentioned in chapter 4, a common form of correlational reflection is pastoral diagnosis. In this practice, clinical and theological sources converge in a diagnostic frame to describe client experience and guide intervention. The pastoral counselor's task is to assess religious themes, spiritual "pathologies," and spiritual dimensions of psychopathology that require treatment. Theological language, spiritual metaphor, and theological interpretations of the role of the pastoral counselor become powerful tools to observe matches between religious/spiritual problems and problems in living. In its clearest form, discernment relies on a religious diagnostic schema that juxtaposes religious and psychotherapeutic language and produces seamless dual diagnoses and clinical strategies.[3] Nancy Ramsay's approach expands pastoral diagnosis beyond traditional categories of pathology to include sensitivity to a broad spectrum of contextual variables.[4] This approach presents a refined and highly conceptual way of reflecting theologically on client assessment, setting goals, and selecting client interventions. However, it also presents several tensions. For example, like any diagnostic schema, it is hierarchical. The client does not have access to psychological and theological knowledge possessed by the professional pastoral counselor. Like medical diagnosis, pastoral reflection becomes a professional activity that rarely invites the client into full participation. This can objectify clients, participate in diagnostic reductionism, support medical and psychological assumptions that oppress clients, and disconnect theological reflection from the broader life of faith communities.

Correlation is also expressed by what Don Browning called a "revised correlational method." This method is not as common as pastoral diagnosis or formational methods. It assumes that deep metaphors in counseling theory and client experience are theological and express moral visions for human life. Discernment takes place through conversations that examine information from common human experience (psychotherapy, client experience, counselor experience, social context) and theology. This conversation explores competing visions of human life and well-being. It compares the implicit religious metaphors, theories of obligation, rules and roles expressed by theory, theology, and client/counselor experience. These are judged against an "inner core of morality"[5] that is independent of both religious and psychotherapeutic paradigms. Through this process of discernment, pastoral counselors can form a composite moral vision of the human person that avoids depending on any one psychotherapeutic theory, diagnostic schema, or any one therapist's or client's experience. This is useful to help clients organize their lives toward new experience and expanded moral ends.

This second form of correlation helps counselors who face competing theological, theoretical, and experiential information. Its strength is also its practical liability. It is complex and founded in moral philosophy and theological ethics, which may discourage some pastoral counselors. In addition, the link between reflection and clinical action can become remote as conversations become highly philosophical. Like formation and diagnosis motifs, this form of reflection is hierarchical and assumes that the counselor's knowledge is more important than the client's indigenous knowledge. Most pastoral counselors who use this method believe it is worth the effort and produces valuable, nonreductionistic information for treatment and the broader life of the church.

Liberation motifs begin with attention to social location and the therapist's and client's embodied experience. They stay grounded in concrete, particular events with the goal of recovering the gospel in a context of suffering. Liberation methods are very personal and decenter clinical decision making and clinical hierarchy. Those who suffer (clients) are not dysfunctional or sick. Instead, suffering is related to specific locations and social structures in which people are objectified, marginalized, unheard, and unseen. Those who seek help are invited into full partnership in active-reflective meaning making that transforms by leading those who are oppressed toward their own empowerment.[6] This motif aims for transformation that improves life and changes social structures. Praxis[7] is the primary task of reflection. It is a constructive method that creates new meaning by giving voice to stories of oppressed or demoralized people in ways that allow these stories to take on new meanings and produce new symbols of hope. Praxis is a special kind of discerning dialogue.

> [Praxis] begins in the belief that God acts in history, is revealed in everyday events, and is not neutral. It proceeds as people of faith circulate through an action-reflection cycle to locate God in the embodied life of oppressed people and then cooperate with God in healing, reconciling, and liberating. In this cycle, the people of God are drawn to God's transforming purposes to change the social institutions, religious structures, values, practices, and policies that keep women, children, and men from human wholeness.... Praxis is more than a way to cause change. It is a way of forming, or *trans*forming, a mutual future that allows a deeper and more challenging knowledge of God for both the oppressed and the oppressor. It is a concrete way of being Christian that is authentically spiritual. It calls us into critical dialogue with the oppressed as a form of prayer, and identifies us as peacemakers in search of shalom.[8]

Liberative motifs warrant close examination because they require that we press the boundaries of religious and psychotherapeutic tradition in order to interpret God's radically inclusive love in contexts of individual, family, or community pain. Clients are not "wounded others" but those by whom we ourselves will be changed. Praxis is a multilevel approach that challenges systems of power and questions dominant cultural narratives that demoralize. It reduces the hierarchy between clients and therapists, avoids technical language, and values client description of experience over therapist interpretation. In its postmodern form it requires that clients are included in all reflective action. Psychotherapeutic knowledge is valued, but not without careful social analysis that is sensitive to how psychotherapy and its procedures can become a form of bondage and oppression. This method often highlights the limitations of both the therapeutic hour and the insulated therapeutic relationship. Neither can contain praxis or hermeneutical circulation, which gives praxis life (figure 1).[9] Hermeneutical circulation begins (step 1) when counselor and client are drawn into a therapeutic story and "jarred" by the client's experience and its relational meaning. Both client and counselor experience the limitations of their understanding (step 2) and turn to conversations with theological sources outside the counseling relationship (step 3). These would include conversations with faith traditions, theological principles, biblical stories, behavioral sciences (as common human experience), and others' personal experience. These conversations broaden horizons (step 4) and present new options that can widen the scope of action in counseling (step 5). As seen in the examples below, this can take place through clients' and therapists' conversations with important others outside of therapy, through expansion of the therapy system, or through in-session consultants and reflecting teams.

The strength of liberation motifs lies in their reduction of hierarchy in therapy, inclusion of the client at all steps of reflection, depathologizing stand toward client problems, and expectations that transformation will include both client and community. Therapeutic use of self and pastoral identity are central in this form of reflection as the therapist brings her or his full humanity to the reflective process. This method also has a broader ability than others to manage plurality of experience, culture, thought, theory, and theology as multiple voices are invited to hermeneutical circulation. It also encourages therapists to diversify and expand their guiding theories and practices. On the other hand, these methods may overestimate clients' ability to engage in the work of praxis. Counselor and client together must assess the client's contexts and capabilities and make decisions about how and where to engage hermeneutical circulation and its practical outcome. By decentering psychological information, client disability may be overlooked. Therapist and client may also misjudge how transformative action may be received by wider social and religious communities and be

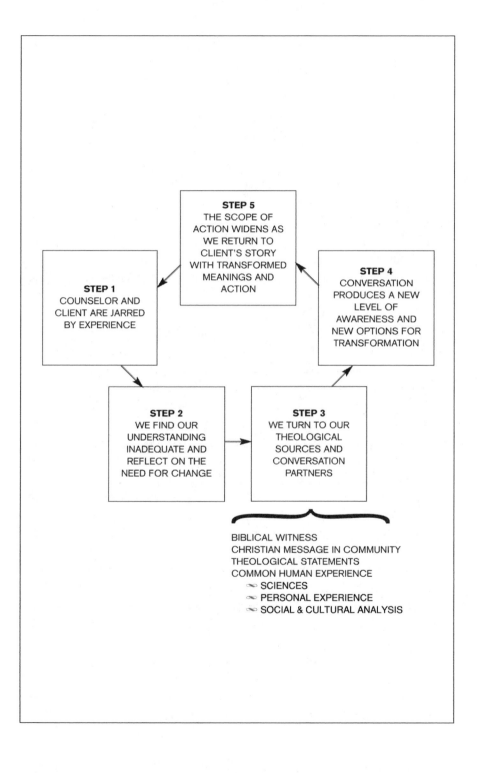

STEP 5
THE SCOPE OF ACTION WIDENS AS WE RETURN TO CLIENT'S STORY WITH TRANSFORMED MEANINGS AND ACTION

STEP 1
COUNSELOR AND CLIENT ARE JARRED BY EXPERIENCE

STEP 4
CONVERSATION PRODUCES A NEW LEVEL OF AWARENESS AND NEW OPTIONS FOR TRANSFORMATION

STEP 2
WE FIND OUR UNDERSTANDING INADEQUATE AND REFLECT ON THE NEED FOR CHANGE

STEP 3
WE TURN TO OUR THEOLOGICAL SOURCES AND CONVERSATION PARTNERS

BIBLICAL WITNESS
CHRISTIAN MESSAGE IN COMMUNITY
THEOLOGICAL STATEMENTS
COMMON HUMAN EXPERIENCE
  ∞ SCIENCES
  ∞ PERSONAL EXPERIENCE
  ∞ SOCIAL & CULTURAL ANALYSIS

frustrated by lack of response. Finally, this form of reflection often requires participation by others that may be expensive and hard to organize. The motion of liberative praxis can best be described with a case study.

Hermeneutical Circulation Step 1: Perception and "Jarring"

Mary M. is a thirty-five-year-old Hispanic woman. She is a native of the Pacific Southwest and a second-generation immigrant from Mexico. She has two children from her first marriage, Anna (eight years old) and Raul (six). Ryan, age three, was born to her and Jason, her present husband. Jason is Euro-American and grew up in the Midwest. This is his first marriage. They have been married for four years. Mary's ex-husband lives in a nearby community. He has maintained contact with his children, but child support has been a problem since their divorce six years ago. Mary works full-time as a graphic artist. Jason is struggling to build his business as an insurance agent. Both grew up in working-class families and are the first in their families to earn college degrees. They struggle financially to support a household, pay back college loans, and manage their consumer debt. Mary has felt overwhelmed, sad, and "worn down" for several months. Recently she has awakened almost daily dreading work that she previously loved. Twice in the past week she became so tearful that she could not continue her workday. She has been irritable with Jason and has had little energy for her three children. She consulted Carol D., a pastoral counselor, because she felt that she was "losing it" at work and at home. Carol is a member of a multistaff pastoral counseling center located in the suburbs of a large city. This is Mary's first contact with a counselor of any kind.

In the first session, Carol listened to Mary talk about being a "horrible failure" as a wife, mother, and professional. When Carol asked her what she meant, Mary spoke of being unable to "get it all done." She felt guilty about not being as involved in her children's school as other mothers, cooking only two or three times a week, and being too tired to spend quality time with her husband. Most of all, she felt she did not live up to the kind of mother her own mother had been. She was also distressed that she could not see herself as the "Proverbs 31 woman" advocated by a recent class she attended in her church. Mary confirmed that her feelings of fail-

ure had increased after completing this class, which was led by a respected woman in the congregation. Carol learned that Mary was deeply dedicated to her church (Methodist) and considered herself and Jason committed Christians. She attended worship and classes three times a week and was active in service events. As part of the intake process, Carol administered the SCL-90[10] and the Spiritual Experience Index.[11] These instruments showed that Mary was experiencing a constellation of emotional difficulties and that her religious system was mature, internalized, differentiated, and personally integrated. Carol also discovered that Mary had talked with her physician about her experience but had rejected the idea of antidepressants after they discussed possible benefits and side effects.

Analysis. This story jars our safe therapeutic world. It makes us listen in a different way to pain, marginalization, or demoralization. It troubles us and demands that we join our client's world in hope of empowering subjugated stories that lead toward full humanity. As Carol listened to Mary's story, she was struck (or jarred) by the intensity of Mary's unhappiness and how Mary's emotional life seemed to have capsized at the intersection of religious teaching and her daily life. As a professional woman, woman of faith, wife, and mother of two children herself, Carol was unsettled. She recalled her struggle to balance professional life, children, home, and religious commitments. She also recalled her religious struggle with female images and expectations in her tradition. She was concerned that she might overidentify with Mary, but she also knew she could not be a neutral observer. She was jarred by Mary's story. Once jarred, pastoral counselors must give up their privileged positions and become partners with clients to discover God's presence in this now mutually shared reality. This position encourages pastoral counselors to assess clients in ways that affirm shared humanity while attending also to problems that may warrant particular kinds of diagnoses. It also mitigates pastoral counselors against using diagnosis in a way that relegates clients to impersonal categories. This position also requires careful attention to power differences between the counselor and the client. Therapists who are blind to or deny the power they wield as socially (or religiously) appointed experts can exploit or abuse clients.

Hermeneutical Circulation Step 2: Expanding Perception

In the second session, Carol wondered with Mary about conflicting demands in her life. What did God expect of women? What did culture demand of women, especially working moms? Did not getting it all done constitute failure? How did these fit together? She and Mary talked and wondered together about what they were not seeing. They also agreed that both Mary and Carol might benefit from information from some other sources.

Analysis. In step 2, both counselor and client discover the limitations of knowledge they bring to the problem, reflect on the need for change, and take steps to expand their perception. The pastoral counselor can now "lock eyes" (pastoral presence) with the client in a way that forces hard questions about God's radical demand for inclusion, our own ideological captivity, our complicity in the client's pain, and the meaning of justice in this specific, embodied location. This engagement forces us to release preconceived notions about therapy outcomes and what we "know" about the client and his or her circumstances through intuition and theory. These are replaced by a commitment to listen to, learn about, and risk being transformed by what the counselor may discover in this new territory.

Hermeneutical Circulation Step 3: Turning to Sources with New Questions

At the end of the second session, Carol asked Mary if she was willing to do some homework. Would she be willing to look more closely at her experience and her church's teaching about women? Mary agreed to keep a log of her daily activities and journal feelings she had about the log. She would also schedule time to talk with her pastor about her response to the workshop on the "Proverbs 31 woman." Carol determined that her own homework would be to talk with a consultant to assure she did not over-identify with Mary. She asked Mary's permission to speak with some of her professional colleagues about their work together and promised to

bring a report to the next session about what she learned from this conversation. Mary agreed and expressed appreciation for Carol's investment in her life.

Analysis. By using homework and including Mary in decision making about consultation, Carol is defining therapy as a mutual investment, beginning to organize a guiding rationale for treatment, shaping preliminary rituals, and modeling hope. Carol realizes that her own social location is important in the process. Her motivation to consult colleagues is dual: to broaden her perception of Mary and her experience and to test her use of self. She will want to identify how her history, experience, and social location interact with Mary's history and experience. She will also want to explore areas of captivity to cultural, theoretical, or class-related ideology. Her introduction of a broader, consultative therapeutic community affirms how seriously she takes Mary's story and lays the foundation for expanding the treatment system in more communal and contextual ways.

Carol introduced Mary to her colleagues at a regularly scheduled case conference. Her primary question was how much self-disclosure was appropriate. She felt deeply drawn to share some of her own experience as a working mother, stepfamily survivor, and woman. At the same time, she worried that this may be an expression of her own need rather than entirely in service to Mary's need. Could she share and keep Mary's therapy central? She and her colleagues explored her motivation, what she might disclose, and what she hoped Mary would gain from her disclosure. Carol observed that Mary seemed to benefit most from a blend of emotion-based and collaborative empathy. She responded best when the counselor and client collaborated around homework, but this seemed dependent upon Carol "truly feeling" Mary's emotional experience. Carol thought sharing parts of her own struggle could be helpful. Angela K., a Korean-American therapist, urged caution. She reminded Carol of ethnic and class differences that mitigated assuming too much similarity between Carol's story and Mary's. How would Carol distinguish what parts of her story were empowering? Carol had grown up in an upper-middle-class family with Euro-American privilege and held a PhD in pastoral

counseling. How would she sort this out? Angela thought some sharing could model hope, but too many assumptions of familiarity or similarity could disempower and demoralize Mary. She also thought attending to Mary's Hispanic heritage and Mujerista theology[12] could have a positive effect in therapy. Mary was religiously involved, spiritually aware, intelligent, and enthusiastic about collaborative exercises. Could Carol build on this by introducing ethnic and theological issues? David R. suggested that Carol ask Mary's permission to videotape a session and present it at their next theological reflection group.

When Carol and Mary met for their third session, Mary had completed her log and journal. She had not been able to schedule time with her pastor until the following week. Mary reviewed her log. It showed very long days, multiple church commitments, and an abundance of household chores. When Mary finished, Carol sighed and told Mary she felt overwhelmed just by listening to what Mary had done during the week. She wondered if anyone could maintain that level of work and stay healthy. Mary talked about what it felt like to keep the log—she felt more overwhelmed than ever and frustrated that she could see nothing to change. Carol asked Mary to change her log for the following week. She would log messages she got from the media, the people around her, her recollections from her personal history, and her church that instructed her about how she should manage life as mother, wife, and professional woman. She would also interview an older woman she had mentioned as one who modeled balance in her work, church, and marital life. Carol's assignment for herself was to look for "data" about women's workloads and emotional health. She also discussed videotaping their next session and reviewing the tape with her colleagues. Carol promised to bring detailed input from the consultation to the following session. Mary was fascinated with this idea and agreed.

In the fourth session—which was videotaped—Mary shared that she felt vastly overwhelmed. She had logged images from television, newspapers, and magazines that showed perfectly dressed, trim, beautifully made-up women carrying kids to preschool in clean minivans, who then smiled their way to work and later enjoyed a pleasant romantic dinner with their husbands. That was certainly not her world. She also summarized her talk with Joanne, the woman who "had it all together." Joanne, she discovered, felt as overwhelmed as Mary but was better at "smiling." She recounted how she had taken medication for depression through most of her children's childhood and adolescence. Her marriage had been chron-

ically on the edge of divorce from never-resolved conflicts around work schedules and household responsibilities. Looking back, Joanne was able to "hang in there" for her children, but she also lives with lingering resentment about chronic depression, long hours, and lack of recognition for the sacrifices she made to see her children successfully off to college. Mary was stunned by Joanne's truthfulness. The following day, she had met with her pastor who responded with feeling but offered little help. Mary was frustrated by his "God will give you strength to endure attitude" and his offer to pray with her for strength. She thought this was an overly simple response. She appreciated his offer and felt supported in a "certain way," but his response also made her feel like a defective Christian. She had been praying for months, "believing with faith," that things would change, and they had not. Carol affirmed Mary's feelings. She also wondered if praying for strength was really the issue, or was there something else they were not yet seeing? She shared her own homework with Mary: national polls showed that working women put in just as many hours on the job as men, but also did twice as much work to maintain a household as their husbands. Women were twice as likely as men to be diagnosed as depressed and prescribed medication. Furthermore, stepfamily literature showed that she was living in a complex family that was more difficult to manage than a first-married family. Mary pondered for several minutes and said, "At first I felt relieved that I may not be crazy and other women feel these things. But now I'm mad and scared. Knowing this stuff doesn't change anything. It might be easier if I really was crazy. At least I could do something about that. Now I feel like there's no escape." Carol helped Mary become more specific about her feelings. She was angry (and then guilty) with her children for demanding so much, at her church for "just expecting" she will be there, at work because she seemed to do more than others who were less responsible, and fearful that nothing would ever change.

Carol presented her case to the theological reflection group that met biweekly at her center. The group consisted of three pastoral counselors, one marriage and family therapist, a psychologist, and a parish pastor with a doctorate in theology who acted as a theological consultant. The group used a structured framework for reflection[13] that progressed through ten minutes of a shared meditation, a five-minute introduction of the client and therapist, ten minutes in which participants claimed their biases and predispositions about the client(s), and forty minutes in which the group discussed preselected sections of the videotape. The reflection

time closed with a ten-minute discussion of group process. Group mem-
bers were individually assigned to attend to particular voices that spoke
to the clinical situation: voices from scripture, religious traditions, psy-
chotherapy and behavioral sciences, and cultural context. One member
was assigned as a group process observer. The group completed their med-
itation, and Carol started the videotape and briefly introduced Mary. The
group then shared initial personal reactions that might influence their
responses. David, a pastoral counselor, owned his reaction: "I want to feel
for her and make things better. I look at her and she seems so tired and
alone." The group talked a few minutes about how this drew David into a
caring relationship but could also replay patriarchy and disempower
Mary. Erik, a psychologist, noted his impression that Mary was
depressed. He wondered if she should be seen at all without medication.
The group discussed their bias toward medical answers to problems that
could also be deeply embedded in the client's social context.
"Nevertheless," said Erik, "you have to weigh the client's desire to choose
over good clinical practice. It may not be responsible to treat her if she
won't take medication." "I'm struck by Mary's dark skin," said Angela, a
Korean-American pastoral counselor. "I wonder about her story as an
immigrant, what kind of prejudice she faces on her job, what it is like for
her to marry an Anglo, and what kind of family dynamics that brings up
in her extended family."

The group spent the next forty minutes watching and discussing sec-
tions of the videotape. All participants were careful to give voice not only
to their own reactions but also from their assigned perspective. Angela,
who was to reflect from the perspective of cultural context, expressed sur-
prise that Carol had not yet talked with Mary about Mexican American
cultural values, meanings, and expectations and how these affected her
marriage, parenting, and work. Carol responded that she was uncertain
how to bring up the subject and had been waiting for Mary to initiate that
conversation. The group talked about the client's and the therapist's
responsibility for initiative. Angela took a strong stand that it was the
counselor's responsibility to ask hard questions and open dialogue in new
directions. Erik disagreed, but admitted that his theory of counseling
relied on the client to direct conversation. Angela stated that she believed
it was an ethical responsibility to address ethnic and cultural issues that
played a role in client pain. Carol agreed with Angela and stated that she
was hesitant because she did not know much about Mujerista theology
and did not want to force feminist thought onto her client. The group dis-

cussed how theological analysis and new thoughts could be introduced into therapy without "proselytizing" the client. Together, with the help of Joe, their theological consultant, they discussed Mujerista theology and ways it could be introduced with integrity into Carol and Mary's talks. One approach would be for Carol to relay the group's idea that this theology might be helpful but that Carol knew little about it. Therapy could be collaborative as Mary and Carol learned together. Carol reflected that Mary was bright, spiritually aware, and theologically interested. She was likely to be interested in reading and discussing how her ethnicity and family heritage might play a role in her distress. Amy, a family therapist, noted that Carol had talked with Mary briefly about stepfamily issues but had not followed through by exploring how marriage, stepfamily, and religious expectations of family life related to Mary's pain. The group also discussed several theological themes that occurred to them as they listened to the videotape. Mary was working very hard. Joe suggested that she may be driven by "works righteousness." She might benefit from a deeper understanding of grace and God's love. Was Mary struggling with an American culture that valued her only as an object for menial work? Amy wondered whether Mary had any option but to work hard toward her family's "salvation." Was there any space for grace in her life? Would a vulnerable family fail without her work? These questions led to discussion about justice. Was Mary forced to make up for others who underfunctioned? How much was Mary working to make up for gaps left by her ex-husband and present husband? Joe remembered the gospel story of Mary and Martha and wondered whether this Mary was trapped in a present-day "Martha's dilemma." Was she "stuck in the kitchen resenting it" while others got the better deal? Carol left the reflecting team with a number of new questions for therapy. She wrote a brief summary of the group's observations and questions to share with Mary in the next session.

Analysis. The group met regularly to talk about "jarring" cases and listen to multiple theological voices that might have something to say about a case. They began by listening to these voices without drawing conclusions about the client or about therapy. Information from their conversation would travel back into counseling sessions where the client and counselor would evaluate voices and decide how to use new information. Together, client and therapist would explore disempowering narratives and consider new narratives with greater hope.

Hermeneutical Circulation Steps 4 and 5: New Options and Transformed Action

Mary began session five by asking Carol about the videotape and reflection group. Carol shared that the group affirmed Mary's hard work to support her family, but they were also concerned that she was carrying a very heavy load. She then outlined three points she had taken from the group: (1) The team wondered how her Mexican American heritage affected her family expectations, feelings about her divorce, her remarriage, and her level of determination. Furthermore the team had suggested that the two of them might read and discuss some Hispanic women who were theologians and specialized in talking about being Hispanic, female, and American. (2) The team wondered about how she experienced God's love in her life and where she found grace in her daily life. The Proverbs 31 story placed value on work and productivity, but there were many other stories about how women were valued. Carol wondered if finding some of these might be helpful. (3) The team wondered about Mary's relationship with her husband and the fact that she lived in a stepfamily. These were important factors they had not yet discussed, and Carol asked if Mary thought they might have an important place in her pain.

Mary was silent for several minutes. She then stated that she felt overwhelmed by the team's input. All three of these things were very close to her heart. She hadn't known how to bring up her Mexican American heritage with an Anglo therapist, so she had stayed silent, thinking it might not be important. She did not know theologians even thought about Hispanic women and liked the idea of exploring this. She also had deep feelings about both Jason and her ex-husband but was afraid to talk about them. She did not want another divorce, and if she started talking about her anger with Jason, she was afraid she would become so upset she could no longer be a good wife. She had been trying to manage her frustration with Jason through her daily prayer. If she talked about her ex-husband and admitted her deep feelings, she was afraid she would be a "complaining ex-wife" and a spiritual failure. She was intrigued about finding other Bible stories for her life as a woman and wife besides Proverbs 31. She looked forward to talking about that. Carol and Mary discussed how they would proceed. Mary thought her relationship with Jason was most important. Together they decided that Jason should be invited to therapy. Mary was certain he would agree. Mary also wanted to begin talking about her Hispanic heritage. Carol promised to look into Mujerista theology in the next week and would be prepared to talk with Mary about it and suggest some mutual reading. With a bit of mischievous delight, Mary wondered how Carol would manage the Spanish. Carol assured her there were English versions.

Analysis. In this session Carol closed the loop on step 3 of hermeneutical circulation. She added the diverse voices of her own reflective process into her conversations/reflection with Mary. Together they considered them and entered step 4 of hermeneutical circulation as both gained new awareness and explored new options for transformation. Carol and Mary entered step 5 conditionally as the scope of action broadened by inviting Jason into sessions and by agreeing to explore *Mujerista* theology and Mary's Hispanic heritage. As they lived through new conversations and transformation, they might again be jarred in a way that recapitulated the reflective cycle.

Reflecting Team Alternative. Praxis and hermeneutical circulation are practices of a reflective community and can be used in numerous ways. In the case study above, Carol could have created more distance between the client experience and therapy action by limiting reflection to herself and the client. In this case, she would eliminate the extensive use of consultants and turn to personal reading, internal reflection, and identification of her own ideological and cultural captivity. She would engage Mary as a partner, and together the two would listen for multiple voices and follow much the same process. On the other hand, Carol could also move theological reflection into a more communal context that stays closely related to experience by using a reflecting team approach.

A reflecting team is a consultation procedure developed by postmodern, collaborative family therapists.[14] It is based on the work of Gregory Bateson[15] and Humberto Maturana.[16] It assumes that a person's picture of the world forms the foundation of her or his attitudes about that world. Maturana focuses on the idea that there is not a single, or universal, reality. Instead, reality is multiversal—

there are many possible meanings of experience, and many possible pictures of the world and experience in it. People get "stuck" in painful realities when their pictures of the world contain too much repeated "sameness" and too few differences. They become stuck because they have no options for seeing their world differently, changing their attitude toward it, or interacting with it in a new way. However, when two people share their pictures, each can perceive a difference and receive a new version of "reality." Change takes place when perception of difference influences a shift in an individual's vision of and attitude toward his or her world. Bateson calls this a "difference which makes a difference."[17] Tom Andersen,[18] a reflecting team pioneer, notes that therapists must be aware of three levels of difference: a difference too small to be noticed, a difference big enough to be noticed, and a difference that could have a disorganizing effect for clients. Optimally, a reflecting team will facilitate differences big enough to notice but not to disorganize the client or her or his social system.

Using reflecting team procedures, Carol's intervention would change in several ways. She would again talk with Mary about the benefits of consultation and getting other people's point of view about her problem and their work together in therapy. However, rather than asking Mary for permission to present a videotape to her colleagues, Carol would invite her to meet the team of consultants and to work for one session behind a one-way mirror. She would prepare Mary by explaining procedures and expected outcomes. Carol would then organize the team by selecting three colleagues to be consultants. Instead of rigidly structuring voices from theology, theory, or culture, she would select her team with careful attention to their sensitivity to client experience, openness to a variety of interpersonal experience, and their flexibility in perceiving and communicating diverse cultural, spiritual, theological, and theoretical viewpoints. She would count on each consultant's pastoral identity and therapeutic experience to discern how to highlight important differences that were "big enough" but did not threaten disorganization. As in the case study, the theological reflecting team would begin by sharing a meditation.[19] Before the session, Carol and the team would decide how the session would be interrupted for reflection. Carol has the option of interrupting the session after twenty to thirty minutes or allowing the team to decide when to interrupt because they were ready to reflect.

Once behind the one-way mirror, Carol will engage Mary in a therapeutic conversation until breaking for reflection. During the session the team will listen quietly, each person constructing his or her own ideas about what is being seen and heard. Carol can transition to team reflection by asking Mary, for instance, "I wonder if our team has anything to say about our conversation?" At that time the team members change places with Carol and Mary so that they can converse with Mary and Carol watching and listening. They will keep in mind that their task is to generate new visions and ideas, not to find answers or solutions. Team members will spontaneously offer their observations and ideas about the problem and the process of therapy. Comments are related directly to what the team observed in the session and might be more personalized forms of the kinds of questions asked in the case conference above, for example: "I may be wrong, but I wonder about how Mary's Hispanic heritage influences how she thinks about her family and work?" or "I'm struck by how hard Mary seems to be working and how deeply she feels about being a faithful Christian woman. I wonder what Bible stories have influenced her? I wonder how she would feel about stories other than Proverbs 31 that don't tie a woman's worth to work, like Jesus' conversation with Martha in Luke 10 (38-42)?" In the reflecting team, consultants would generate ideas from multiple theological sources that would create a difference (but not a disorienting difference) and avoid absolutist, either-or thinking. Ideas would be presented as possibilities that Mary and Carol can accept or reject. Once the team members have offered their thoughts, Mary and Carol are invited to respond. The scope of reflection broadens again as they discuss their reactions with the team. Carol and Mary will use information from the reflecting team to enrich subsequent therapy sessions.

Reflecting teams can be hard to organize apart from counseling centers with staff available for consultation. However, they hold great potential for expanding the role of theological reflection in pastoral counseling and keeping reflection close to the client's experience and the action of therapy.

Ethical Reflection

Theological reflection is also ethical reflection. When pastoral counselors think theologically about their cases, they also necessarily reflect on how human life should be valued and organized in relationship to the dilemmas, tensions, and competing goods that arise in life. Pastoral counselors must reflect at several ethical levels. At the most basic level pastoral counselors follow rules for ethical behavior established by the American Association of Pastoral Counselors (see appendix for the AAPC Code of Ethics) and other professional groups. These codes protect the public from basic forms of counselor exploitation. They protect the field from unethical pastoral counselors and provide a structure through which counselors can evaluate their practices. Most counselors learn basic ethical requirements in the first weeks of clinical training. Understanding principles and practices of informed consent, respecting confidentiality, maintaining appropriate sexual, financial, and social boundaries, honoring contracts, and not practicing beyond one's competence are foundations that anchor practice. However, codified rules do not insulate pastoral counselors from the inherent complexity of being human, religious (or spiritual), culturally bound, and in relationships with clients, colleagues, and communities. It is beyond the scope of this chapter to list the many ethical questions, problems, and dilemmas facing pastoral counselors. It is more important to point to a code of ethics and insist that pastoral counselors know it and follow it. It is equally important to point to the fact that pastoral practice is permeated with questions of justice, competing goods, and occasions when communities, clients, and colleagues risk exploitation. Codes often fall short in guiding discernment. For this, pastoral counselors must extend theological reflection to include intentional analysis of ethical concerns.

More than thirty years ago, Don Browning proposed that all pastoral care and counseling took place in a moral context.[20] For Browning, the purpose of theological reflection is to engage "hermeneutical rationality" in the face of ethical problems that confront pastoral practice. Reflection moves through five levels and must produce a normative vision of the human life cycle that guides care. The highest level, the metaphorical level, explores ultimate questions such as "in what kind of world or universe do we live?" Psychological or cultural metaphors of ultimate existence that compete for moral value must be compared to Christian images of God as creator, governor, and redeemer. At the second, or obligational, level, reflection asks: "Given this vision of the universe, what are we obligated to do?" Here, pastoral counselors would develop specific propositions about moral behavior and test these against the principle that moral behavior is rational, acts reversibly (do unto others as you would have them do unto you), and is impartial. Competing visions of obligation (for instance, individualism's concern with self-satisfaction) would be compared with Christian symbols of God's impartial love and justice. Browning's third, or tendency-need, level of reflection, asks the question: "Which of our human tendencies and needs are we morally justified in satisfying?" "Facts" from social and psychological theory are brought into conversation with the Christian witness where they are sorted and prioritized through a Christian vision of the human person gained from the metaphorical and obligational reflection. At the contextual-predictive (fourth) level of reflection decisions made by the first three levels are correlated to sociological, psychological, and cultural contexts. At the final (rule-role) level of reflection, pastoral counselors would use the information from levels one through four to help clients organize rules and roles for rational moral living. Rules and roles demanded by popular culture, for instance, are compared with rules and roles suggested by a normative Christian understanding of human life.

Doing justice to Browning's method in a few introductory lines is hard. It is anchored firmly in moral philosophy and deserves careful reading in its own right.[21] Though it can be complex and may intimidate pastoral counselors in daily practice, it is a useful way to make decisions based on clear ethical theory. However, Browning's model is also anchored in a set of assumptions that are problematic for postmodern theologians, some forms of Reformed theology, and postmodern therapists. It is a way of thinking that assumes universal knowledge and locates morality in a personal, individual, rational "self" that makes decisions. According to theologian James McClendon,[22] this "decisionism" is a culture-bound development of Northern European philosophy. It was shaped by Emmanuel Kant's universalizing definition of morality, encouraged by William

James's notion that "will" is the center of the human self, and confirmed by Puritan, pietistic, and revivalistic emphasis on Christians' interior life. According to McClendon, decisionism is a distinct product of a particular cultural era—the modern West—and its overvaluing of volunteerism and interiorization. It provides a misleading normative image of moral life in which all Christians (or humans for that matter) are continuously divided souls forced to make constant decisions about right and wrong.

McClendon calls for narrative ethics as an alternative to decisionism. Christians, for example, participate in a common story. They are bound together by moral convictions about God, neighbor, self, community, and the meaning of past and future. These structure moral life in a way that transcends and is more complex than individual decision making. For McClendon, ethics must address three interlocking narratives: "1) . . . the world of the embodied self in its organic continuity with all nature; 2) . . . the world of custom, covenant, law, practice, and social roles . . . ; and 3) . . . the new world in formation, revised and under revision by the Spirit and power of the risen Christ."[23] Human and Christian life is structured and given meaning through biblical, historical, and contemporary narrative. Character, virtue, convictions, and ethical practices are defined by narratives through which people live. Narrative ethics does not focus on decision making based on a universal principle. Instead, it seeks to discover, understand, and creatively transform a shared, lived story. For the Christian community this will focus on *"Jesus of Nazareth and the kingdom he proclaims—a story that on its moral side requires such discovery, such understanding, and such transformation to be true to itself."*[24] Martin Luther King Jr.'s vision for the beloved community in the context of the American struggle for civil rights and Desmond Tutu's ubuntu theology as it found life in his leadership of the Truth and Reconciliation Commission and resistance to apartheid provide significant examples of narrative ethics. Examples of narrative ethics in pastoral counseling can be found in Archie Smith's[25] relational ethic grounded in Black church experience, Christie Neuger's[26] orientation to therapy with women, and Larry Graham's[27] psychosystemic frame for counseling.

Narrative ethics and liberative praxis can be a strong foundation for ethical reflection. Instead of looking to resolve ethical problems through individual will, narrative ethics bases decisions in a community and its understanding of embodiment, culture, and the future to guide right behavior. A pastoral counselor jarred by an ethical question will prompt hermeneutical circulation. For instance, Carol's concern about personal disclosure in the session could initiate a cycle of reflection (step 1). She was "stuck" partly because there are no clear rules about how much to self-disclose in therapy, and there are varying theoretical approaches to self-disclosure. When she found her understanding inadequate for the circumstances (step 2), she turned to sources beyond herself (beginning step 3). She could have pursued a full cycle of reflection had she extended her question beyond the simple decision of how much of her personal life to disclose to Mary. In step 3 she could explore elements of the Christian narrative that affirm common embodied humanity between her and Mary. Does our Christian faith justify such clear distinctions between self and other? As Carol and Mary explore *Mujerista* theology, should sharing include Carol confronting her own collusion with social realities that subjugate Mary as a Hispanic woman? How would such confession and reconciliation fit into the framework of therapy? What does the gospel witness suggest about this kind of mutual sharing? When a position of "professional distance" is claimed are other faith values at stake? How might joining together in the communion of a shared narrative of Christian women be empowering? What limits to historic narratives of prophet, priest, and wise person project into practices of pastoral engagement? What eschatological vision is expressed if Carol and Mary do or do not share stories and meanings? What Christian practices are at stake? For instance, what is the place of baptism and Communion that equalizes humanity and reminds us that all hope of transformation is from God? Is sharing a common table and baptism a practice that extends into therapy? Carol and her reflecting group could extend this by exploring cultural and social practices. For instance, does collaboration mean something different to a Hispanic Christian woman than to a Euro-American woman? Ultimately, Carol will need to find a way to guide her practices in session with Mary. This model of reflection reminds pastoral counselors that none of our decisions are free from personal and cultural bias. They are all narrative bound. Even our "most cherished and tenaciously held convictions might be false and are in principle always subject to rejection, reformulation, improvement, or reformation."[28] Carol's reflective process broadens her perspective and gives her the ability to be guided by Christian practices. It also influences that community and its practices of care and counseling. She and her community are transformed through the process of reflection.

Conclusion

Pastoral counselors reflect theologically and ethically. This is a grounding practice that transcends therapy model or any set of counseling procedures. It is near the heart of what makes identity and practices pastoral. At its best, it is a form of spiritual practice that holds diverse pastoral counselors together across a multiverse of practices, theories, and personalities that characterize contemporary pastoral counseling.

Notes

1. Several of these motifs are also described in Loren Townsend, "Theological Reflection, Pastoral Counseling, and Supervision," *Journal of Pastoral Theology* 12, no. 1 (2002).

2. Theologian David Tracy uses the notion of common human experience to refer to sciences, literature, and one's experience in the world. Events of everyday life, including events in counseling, are part of common human experience. David Tracy, *Blessed Rage for Order* (New York: Seabury, 1975).

3. Donald D. Denton, *Religious Diagnosis in a Secular Society* (Lanham, Md.: University Press of America, 1986); Nancy Ramsay, *Pastoral Diagnosis: A Resource for Ministries of Care and Counseling* (Minneapolis: Fortress Press, 1998).

4. Ramsay, *Pastoral Diagnosis: A Resource for Ministries of Care and Counseling.*

5. Don S. Browning, *Religious Thought and the Modern Psychologies* (Minneapolis: Fortress Press, 1987/2004), 187.

6. Paulo Freire, *Pedagogy of the Oppressed* (New York: Continuum Press, 1993).

7. For a more complete discussion of praxis, see Robert M. Brown, *Theology in a New Key: Responding to Liberation Themes* (Philadelphia: Westminster Press, 1978); Freire, *Pedagogy of the Oppressed;* Gustavo Gutierrez, *A Theology of Liberation* (Maryknoll, N.Y.: Orbis Books, 1980); Loren L. Townsend, *Pastoral Care with Stepfamilies: Mapping the Wilderness* (St. Louis: Chalice Press, 2000).

8. Townsend, *Pastoral Care with Stepfamilies: Mapping the Wilderness,* 41.

9. See: *Theology in a New Key: Responding to Liberation Themes* and Robert McAfee Brown, *Unexpected News: Reading the Bible with Third World Eyes* (Philadelphia: Westminster Press, 1984).

10. Symptom Checklist-90. See http://www.drjunno.com/scl90.pdf and http://www.hsrd.research.va.gov/for_researchers/measurement/instrument/

instrument_reviews2.cfm?detail=43. An updated version may be purchased at http://www.pearsonassessments.com/tests/scl90r.htm.

11. V. Genia, "The Spiritual Experience Index: A Measure of Spiritual Maturity," *Journal of Religion and Health* 30 (1991).

12. See Ada Maria Isasi-Diaz, *Mujerista Theology: A Theology for the Twenty-first Century* (Maryknoll, N.Y.: Orbis, 1996). Mujerista theology begins in the struggle of Hispanic women in the United States against ethnic prejudice, sexism, and classism. It engages liberative praxis to help Hispanic women understand oppressive structures that stereotype, abuse, and dehumanize them and determine the course of their daily lives. Mujerista theology helps Hispanic women find and affirm God's presence in their daily lives and communities. It also insists that they are central to defining a different, or preferred, future for themselves and society. This is partly accomplished by enabling Hispanic women to understand how much they have internalized their own oppression by complying with prevailing social systems. Change will take place only as they themselves change and resist resignation to the suffering and self-effacement assigned to them by the dominant American culture.

13. Loren Townsend, "Creative Theological Imagining," *Journal of Pastoral Care* 50, no. 4 (1996).

14. Steven Friedman, ed., *The Reflecting Team in Action: Collaborative Practice in Family Therapy, Guilford Family Therapy Series* (New York: Guilford Press, 1995).

15. Gregory Bateson, *Mind and Nature: A Necessary Unity* (New York: Dutton, 1979); Gregory Bateson, *Steps to an Ecology of Mind* (New York: Ballantine, 1972).

16. Humberto R. Maturana, "The Biology of Language: The Epistemology of Reality," in *Psychology and Biology of Language and Thought*, eds. G. Miller and E. Lenneberg (New York: Academic Press, 1978).

17. Bateson, *Steps to an Ecology of Mind*, 453.

18. Tom Andersen, "The Reflecting Team: Dialogue and Meta-Dialogue in Clinical Work," *Family Process* 26 (1987).

19. Rationale for meditation (Townsend, "Creative Theological Imagining") is to help the team open an analogical perceptual framework for the session. A meditative exercise is meant to stimulate the inner life of the team. "Meditative reflection facilitates a different kind of knowing. Personal connections apprehended through the right brain stimulate analogical, or 'mini-kairos,' understandings of 'complex totalities' which are immediately and irrationally present for the therapist and the group. 'The whole' is known through 'the part' that is observed. This meditative reflection is a way of listening and structuring perception receptively. It is capable of stimulating deep areas of religious imagery and life struggle for the therapist and reflection group" (354).

20. Don S. Browning, *The Moral Context of Pastoral Care* (Philadelphia: Westminster Press, 1976); Don S. Browning, *Religious Ethics and Pastoral Care* (Philadelphia: Fortress Press, 1983); Browning, *Religious Thought and the Modern Psychologies*.

21. See especially Browning, *Religious Ethics and Pastoral Care*.

22. James W. McClendon, *Systematic Theology: Ethics* (Nashville: Abingdon Press, 1986).

23. Ibid., 67.

24. Ibid., 332, italics in original.

25. Archie Smith, *The Relational Self.*

26. Christie Cozad Neuger, *Counseling Women.*

27. Larry Graham, *Core of Persons, Core of Worlds: A Psychosystems Approach* (Nashville: Abingdon Press, 1992).

28. James W. McClendon and James M. Smith, *Understanding Religious Convictions* (South Bend, Ind.: University of Notre Dame Press, 1975), 118.

American Association of Pastoral Counselors Code of Ethics

Code is reprinted with permission.[1] It is currently under revision. Updates can be obtained at www.aapc.org/content/ethics.

Principle I—Prologue

As members[2] of the American Association of Pastoral Counselors, we are committed to the various theologies, traditions, and values of our faith communities and to the dignity and worth of each individual. We are dedicated to advancing the welfare of those who seek our assistance and to the maintenance of high standards of professional conduct and competence. We are accountable for our ministry whatever its setting. This accountability is expressed in relationships to clients, colleagues, students, our faith communities, and through the acceptance and practice of the principles and procedures of this Code of Ethics.

In order to uphold our standards, as members of AAPC we covenant to accept the following foundational premises:

A. To maintain responsible association with the faith group in which we have ecclesiastical standing.
B. To avoid discriminating against or refusing employment, educational opportunity, or professional assistance to anyone on the basis of race, gender, sexual orientation, religion, or national origin; provided that nothing herein shall limit a member or center

from utilizing religious requirements or exercising a religious preference in employment decisions.

C. To remain abreast of new developments in the field through both educational activities and clinical experience. We agree at all levels of membership to continue post-graduate education and professional growth including supervision, consultation, and active participation in the meetings and affairs of the Association.

D. To seek out and engage in collegial relationships, recognizing that isolation can lead to a loss of perspective and judgment.

E. To manage our personal lives in a healthful fashion and to seek appropriate assistance for our own personal problems or conflicts.

F. To diagnose or provide treatment only for those problems or issues that are within the reasonable boundaries of our competence.

G. To establish and maintain appropriate professional relationship boundaries.

Principle II—Professional Practices

In all professional matters members of AAPC maintain practices that protect the public and advance the profession.

A. We use our knowledge and professional associations for the benefit of the people we serve and not to secure unfair personal advantage.

B. We clearly represent our level of membership and limit our practice to that level.

C. Fees and financial arrangements, as with all contractual matters, are always discussed without hesitation or equivocation at the onset and are established in a straight-forward, professional manner.

D. We are prepared to render service to individuals and communities in crisis without regard to financial remuneration when necessary.

E. We neither receive nor pay a commission for referral of a client.

F. We conduct our practice, agency, regional, and Association fiscal affairs with due regard to recognized business and accounting procedures.

G. Upon the transfer of a pastoral counseling practice or the sale of real, personal, tangible, or intangible property or assets used in such practice, the privacy and well being of the client shall be of primary concern.
  1. Client names and records shall be excluded from the transfer or sale.
  2. Any fees paid shall be for services rendered, consultation, equipment, real estate, and the name and logo of the counseling agency.
H. We are careful to represent facts truthfully to clients, referral sources, and third party payors regarding credentials and services rendered. We shall correct any misrepresentation of our professional qualifications or affiliations.
I. We do not malign colleagues or other professionals.

Principle III—Client Relationships

It is the responsibility of members of AAPC to maintain relationships with clients on a professional basis.

A. We do not abandon or neglect clients. If we are unable, or unwilling for appropriate reasons, to provide professional help or continue a professional relationship, every reasonable effort is made to arrange for continuation of treatment with another professional.
B. We make only realistic statements regarding the pastoral counseling process and its outcome.
C. We show sensitive regard for the moral, social, and religious standards of clients and communities. We avoid imposing our beliefs on others, although we may express them when appropriate in the pastoral counseling process.
D. Counseling relationships are continued only so long as it is reasonably clear that the clients are benefiting from the relationship.
E. We recognize the trust placed in and unique power of the therapeutic relationship. While acknowledging the complexity of some pastoral relationships, we avoid exploiting the trust and dependency of clients. We avoid those dual relationships with clients (e.g., business or close personal relationships) which

could impair our professional judgment, compromise the integrity of the treatment, and/or use the relationship for our own gain.

F. We do not engage in harassment, abusive words or actions, or exploitative coercion of clients or former clients.

G. All forms of sexual behavior or harassment with clients are unethical, even when a client invites or consents to such behavior or involvement. Sexual behavior is defined as, but not limited to, all forms of overt and covert seductive speech, gestures, and behavior as well as physical contact of a sexual nature; harassment is defined as but not limited to, repeated comments, gestures, or physical contacts of a sexual nature.

H. We recognize that the therapist/client relationship involves a power imbalance, the residual effects of which are operative following the termination of the therapy relationship. Therefore, all sexual behavior or harassment as defined in Principle III, G with former clients is unethical.

Principle IV—Confidentiality

As members of AAPC we respect the integrity and protect the welfare of all persons with whom we are working and have an obligation to safeguard information about them that has been obtained in the course of the counseling process.

A. All records kept on a client are stored or disposed of in a manner that assures security and confidentiality.

B. We treat all communications from clients with professional confidence.

C. Except in those situations where the identity of the client is necessary to the understanding of the case, we use only the first names of our clients when engaged in supervision or consultation. It is our responsibility to convey the importance of confidentiality to the supervisor/consultant; this is particularly important when the supervision is shared by other professionals, as in a supervisory group.

D. We do not disclose client confidences to anyone, except: as mandated by law; to prevent a clear and immediate danger to someone; in the course of a civil, criminal, or disciplinary action arising from the counseling where the pastoral counselor is a defendant; for purposes of supervision or consultation; or by previously obtained written permission. In cases involving more than one person (as client) written permission must be obtained from all legally accountable persons who have been present during the counseling before any disclosure can be made.

E. We obtain informed written consent of clients before audio and/or video tape recording or permitting third party observation of their sessions.

F. We do not use these standards of confidentiality to avoid intervention when it is necessary, e.g., when there is evidence of abuse of minors, the elderly, the disabled, the physically or mentally incompetent.

G. When current or former clients are referred to in a publication, while teaching or in a public presentation, their identity is thoroughly disguised.

H. We as members of AAPC agree that as an express condition of our membership in the Association, Association ethics communications, files, investigative reports, and related records are strictly confidential and waive their right to use same in a court of law to advance any claim against another member. Any member seeking such records for such purpose shall be subject to disciplinary action for attempting to violate the confidentiality requirements of the organization. This policy is intended to promote pastoral and confessional communications without legal consequences and to protect potential privacy and confidentiality interests of third parties.

Principle V—Supervisee, Student, and Employee Relationships

As members of AAPC we have an ethical concern for the integrity and welfare of our supervisees, students, and employees. These relationships are maintained on a professional and confidential basis. We recognize our influential position with regard to both current and former supervisees, students, and employees, and avoid exploiting their trust and dependency. We make every effort to avoid dual relationships with such persons that could impair our judgment or increase the risk of personal and/or financial exploitation.

A. We do not engage in ongoing counseling relationships with current supervisees, students, and employees.
B. We do not engage in sexual or other harassment of supervisees, students, employees, research subjects, or colleagues.
C. All forms of sexual behavior, as defined in Principle III.G, with our supervisees, students, research subjects, and employees (except in employee situations involving domestic partners) are unethical.
D. We advise our students, supervisees, and employees against offering or engaging in, or holding themselves out as competent to engage in, professional services beyond their training, level of experience, and competence.
E. We do not harass or dismiss an employee who has acted in a reasonable, responsible, and ethical manner to protect, or intervene on behalf of, a client or other member of the public or another employee.

Principle VI—Interprofessional Relationships

As members of AAPC we relate to and cooperate with other professional persons in our community and beyond. We are part of a network of health care professionals and are expected to develop and maintain interdisciplinary and interprofessional relationships.

A. We do not offer ongoing clinical services to persons currently receiving treatment from another professional without prior knowledge of and in consultation with the other professional, with the clients' informed consent. Soliciting such clients is unethical.
B. We exercise care and interprofessional courtesy when approached for services by persons who claim or appear to have inappropriately terminated treatment with another professional.

Principle VII—Advertising

Any advertising by or for a member of AAPC, including announcements, public statements, and promotional activities, is undertaken with the purpose of helping the public make informed judgments and choices.

A. We do not misrepresent our professional qualifications, affiliations, and functions, or falsely imply sponsorship or certification by any organization.
B. We may use the following information to describe ourselves and the services we provide: name; highest relevant academic degree earned from an accredited institution; date, type, and level of certification or licensure; AAPC membership level, clearly stated; address and telephone number; office hours; a brief review of services offered, e.g., individual, couple, and group counseling; fee information; languages spoken; and policy regarding third party payments. Additional relevant information may be provided if it is legitimate, reasonable, free of deception, and not otherwise prohibited by these principles. We may not use the initials "AAPC" after our names in the manner of an academic degree.
C. Announcements and brochures promoting our services describe them with accuracy and dignity, devoid of all claims or evaluation. We may send them to professional persons, religious institutions, and other agencies, but to prospective individual clients only in response to inquiries.
D. We do not make public statements which contain any of the following:
   1. A false, fraudulent, misleading, deceptive, or unfair statement.
   2. A misrepresentation of fact or a statement likely to mislead or deceive because in context it makes only a partial disclosure of relevant facts.
   3. A testimonial from a client regarding the quality of services or products.
   4. A statement intended or likely to create false or unjustified expectations of favorable results.
   5. A statement implying unusual, unique, or one-of-a-kind abilities, including misrepresentation through sensationalism, exaggeration, or superficiality.
   6. A statement intended or likely to exploit a client's fears, anxieties, or emotions.

7. A statement concerning the comparative desirability of offered services.
8. A statement of direct solicitation of individual clients.

E. We do not compensate in any way a representative of the press, radio, television, or other communication medium for the purpose of professional publicity and news items. A paid advertisement must be identified as such, unless it is contextually apparent that it is a paid advertisement. We are responsible for the content of such advertisement. Any advertisement to the public by radio or television is to be pre-recorded, approved by us, and a recording of the actual transmission retained in our possession.

F. Advertisements or announcements by us of workshops, clinics, seminars, growth groups, or similar services or endeavors are to give a clear statement of purpose and a clear description of the experiences to be provided. The education, training, and experience of the provider(s) involved are to be appropriately specified.

G. Advertisements or announcements soliciting research participants, in which clinical or other professional services are offered as an inducement, make clear the nature of the services as well as the cost and other obligations or risks to be accepted by participants in the research.

Notes

1. The AAPC Code of Ethics may be reproduced only after contacting the AAPC Association Office to ensure that the most current copy of the Code can be provided. The Code was amended April 28, 1994. The AAPC Code of Ethics and the Ethics Committee Procedures were separated by action of the AAPC membership on April 17, 1993. The Board of Directors is now authorized to modify ethics committee procedures without further action by the membership. Members should note that the substantive rule from the Code of Ethics to be applied to an alleged violation will continue to be determined by the date of the alleged violation and not the date the complaint is received. However, as a result of the action taken, the current procedures in effect will be followed for all complaints brought after April 17, 1993, regardless of the date of alleged violation.

2. The use of "member," "we," "us," and "our" refers to and is binding upon all levels of individual and institutional membership and affiliation of AAPC.